CALLED TO BE GOD'S OWN

A Salvation Army Christ-based
Approach to Recovery and Salvationism

By Glen Doss

Called to Be God's Own
Glen Doss

Adult Rehabilitation Centers Command
USA Western Territory

All Bible references are NIV unless otherwise stated. Other Bibles used are: J.B. Phillips, KJV and NLT.

Glen Doss
Called to Be God's Own

July 2014

Copyright © The Salvation Army
USA Western Territory

ISBN 978-0-692-22199-0

Printed in the United States

MISSION STATEMENT OF THE SALVATION ARMY

The Salvation Army, an international movement, is an evangelical part of the universal Christian Church. Its message is based on the Bible. Its ministry is motivated by the love of God. Its mission is to preach the gospel of Jesus Christ and to meet human needs in His name without discrimination.

Table of Contents

Introduction

Addiction to drugs, alcohol and other mood altering substances remains an ever mounting scourge within our society. The enticement of intoxication is one of the most powerful influences operating upon the mind of the addicted. It has been many people's experience that *only the power of God himself* can countermand this force.

In light of The Salvation Army's continuing war against this epidemic, Major Man-Hee Chang, adult rehabilitation center commander for the USA Western Territory, requested the development of a unique recovery program for adult rehabilitation center (ARC) beneficiaries, alumni and others in recovery who are seeking membership in The Salvation Army. This program, *Called to Be God's Own*, incorporates the 12 vital areas of the Army's spiritual life highlighted by The Salvation Army's 1999 international spiritual life commission. It draws heavily on Commissioner Robert Street's published report of the commission's findings, *Called to be God's People*.

Called to Be God's Own is a Christ-based approach to recovery, drawing together three elements: the commission's "Call to Salvationists," the doctrines of The Salvation Army (with the *Manual of Salvationism* serving as an invaluable guide), and the 12 steps of Alcoholics Anonymous.

Innumerable addicts and alcoholics will attest that the Holy Spirit used the famous 12-step program as an avenue through which their minds were renewed, setting them free from the compulsion to drink or use drugs. They know through personal experience that if the Trinitarian God of the Bible is their self-proclaimed "Higher Power," then genuine sanctification is the outcome, transforming them increasingly into the character and image of Christ. Some of their stories are told in this volume, though their names have been changed to preserve their anonymity.

We believe the secret behind the incredible success of AA and its many spinoff 12-step programs is that the steps themselves are Biblical commands spelled out in a "user-friendly" format. Scripture emphasizes that consistent compliance with God's direction is the pathway of discipleship. *"If you hold to my teaching,"* explains Jesus, *"you are really my disciples"* (John 8:31).

The evidence is clear that if a person steps out in purposeful obedience to God's commands, he or she will grow spiritually. Such a person, taught Jesus, is *"like a man building a house, who dug down deep and laid the foundation on rock. When a flood came, the torrent struck that house but could not shake it, because it was well built"* (Luke 6:48).

The Salvation Army takes the 12-step program back to its Christian roots. The God of the evangelical Oxford Group, AA's forerunner, was the God of the Bible. He is God in three persons: the Father, Son and Holy Spirit. The 12 steps outline the way to develop a personal relationship with Christ, so that we ultimately harness his power in our lives; hence the proven effectiveness of what is called "working the steps."

A Christ-based 12-step program teaches us first to get right with God, accepting Jesus Christ as our Lord and Savior—steps 1, 2 and 3. Next God helps us get right with ourselves—steps 4 through 7. Then he helps us to get right with others—steps 8 and 9.

Steps 10, 11 and 12 are beautifully crafted instruments through which God helps us monitor our hearts, keeping our walk with him active and current so that we do not fall. *Above all else, guard your heart, for it is the wellspring of life,* teaches wise King Solomon (Prov. 4:23). Steps 10 through 12 guide us in growth as we continue to practice these principles (steps) and pass on to others the message of how Christ set us free.

This is the stated goal of the *Called to Be God's Own* program: That each participant *be thoroughly equipped for every good work* (2 Tim. 3:17) as befits *a good soldier of Jesus Christ* (2 Tim. 2:3). Successful completion of this program may lead to the participant's enrollment as a Salvation Army soldier or adherent.

A Brief History of
The Salvation Army

William Booth embarked upon his ministerial career in 1852, desiring to win the lost multitudes of England to Christ. He walked the streets of London to preach the gospel of Jesus Christ to the poor, the homeless, the hungry, and the destitute.

Booth abandoned the conventional concept of a church and a pulpit, instead taking his message to the people. His fervor led to disagreement with church leaders in London, who preferred traditional methods. As a result, he withdrew from the church and traveled throughout England, conducting evangelistic meetings. His wife, Catherine, could accurately be called a cofounder of The Salvation Army.

In 1865, William Booth was invited to hold a series of evangelistic meetings in the East End of London. He set up a tent in a Quaker graveyard, and his services became an instant success. This proved to be the end of his wanderings as an independent traveling evangelist. His renown as a religious leader spread throughout London, and he attracted followers who were dedicated to fight for the souls of men and women.

Thieves, prostitutes, gamblers, and drunkards were among Booth's first converts to Christianity. To congregations who were desperately poor, he preached hope and salvation. His aim was to lead people to Christ and link them to a church for further spiritual guidance.

Many churches, however, did not accept Booth's followers because of their pasts. So Booth continued giving his new converts spiritual direction, challenging them to save others like themselves. Soon, they too were preaching and singing in the streets as a living testimony to the power of God.

In 1867, Booth had only 10 full-time workers, but by 1874 the number had grown to 1,000 volunteers and 42 evangelists, all serving under the name "The Christian Mission." Booth assumed the title of general superintendent, with his followers calling him "General." Known as the "Hallelujah Army," the converts spread out of the East End of London into neighboring areas and then to other cities.

Booth was reading a printer's proof of the 1878 annual report when he noticed the statement "The Christian Mission is a volunteer army." Crossing out the words "volunteer army," he penned in "Salvation Army." From those words came the basis of the foundation deed of The Salvation Army.

From that point, converts became soldiers of Christ and were known then, as now, as Salvationists. They launched an offensive throughout the British Isles, in some cases facing real battles as organized gangs mocked and attacked them. In spite of violence and persecution, some 250,000 people were converted under the ministry of The Salvation Army between 1881 and 1885.

Meanwhile, the Army was gaining a foothold in the United States. Lieutenant Eliza Shirley left England to join her parents, who had migrated to America earlier in search of work. In 1879, she held the first meeting of The Salvation Army in America, in Philadelphia. The Salvationists were received enthusiastically. Shirley wrote to General Booth, begging for reinforcements. None were available at first. Glowing reports of the work in Philadelphia, however, eventually convinced Booth, in 1880, to send an official group to pioneer the work in America.

The Salvation Army movement expanded rapidly to Canada, Australia, France, Switzerland, India, South Africa, Iceland, and local neighborhood units. Today The Salvation Army is active in virtually every corner of the world.

(excerpted from http://www.salvationarmyusa.org/vsn/history-of-the-salvation-army)

The Call to Salvationists

The Founders of The Salvation Army declared their belief that God raised up our Movement to enter partnership with him in his "great business" of saving the world. We call upon Salvationists worldwide to reaffirm our shared calling to this great purpose, as signified in our name. Salvation begins with conversion to Christ, but it does not end there. The transformation of an individual leads to a transformation of relationships, of families, of communities, of nations. We long for and anticipate with joy the new creation of all things in Christ. Our mission is God's mission. God in love reaches out through his people to a suffering and needy world, a world that he loves. In mission we express in word and deed and through the totality of our lives the compassion of God for the lost.

Our identification with God in this outward movement of love for the world requires a corresponding inward movement from ourselves towards God. Christ says "Come to me" before he says "Go into the world." These two movements are in relation to each other, like breathing in and breathing out. To engage in one movement to the exclusion of the other is the way of death. To engage in both is the way of life. The vitality of our spiritual life as a Movement will be seen and test-ed in our turning to the world in evangelism and service, but the springs of our spiritual life are to be found in our turning to God in worship, in the disciplines of life in the Spirit, and in the study of God's word.

—Commissioner Robert Street, *Called to be God's People*

The commission recognizes and stresses that the spiritual transfor-mation of an individual begins with a brand new life in Christ but by no means ends there. It leads to a change in all relationships of life: of friends, families, communities, even of nations. Likewise, as we work the 12 steps of AA or NA (Narcotics Anonymous), under the tutelage of a Christian sponsor, God takes us on a journey of reconciliation with him, ourselves and others. And as he makes us whole, he ultimately uses us to help make others whole. We become instruments in his hands. What a wonderful God we serve!

Lost in a Pluralistic Society

As she recounted a decades-long history of drinking, using drugs, gambling, theft, and failed relationship after relationship, Alice became glummer and glummer, until her downcast expression finally collapsed into tears. As she wiped her face with the tissues the chaplain handed her, he suggested that she ask God for help.

Alice glanced at him with suspicion. "God?" she said. "I knew you were going to go there. I don't believe in God. There are so many competing religions. For a while I explored Buddhism, but I just can't accept any of these old myths. They're things people made up to make themselves feel better. Yet today I don't know where to turn."

This is the challenge all Christian evangelists face—to present Jesus Christ to a people struggling to make sense of God in a confused, pluralistic society. Nothing describes this situation any better, I believe, than the volume *Alcoholics Anonymous*. "We looked upon this world of warring individuals, warring theological systems, and inexplicable calamity, with deep skepticism. We looked askance at many individuals who claimed to be godly. How could a Supreme Being have anything to do with it all? And who could comprehend a Supreme Being anyhow?"[1]

Since *Alcoholics Anonymous* appeared in 1939, our world has become even more antagonistic toward religion. This is the face of the society in which people struggling with addiction live today and which Christians must confront head on as they present Christ to a hurting people.

The chaplain asked Alice, "Have you hit on any human remedy at all for your condition?"

She puzzled over this for a moment, then hesitantly said, "No. I am convinced there is none."

"Then you may have to turn to the superhuman," he told her. A look of full acceptance gradually materialized upon her frightened face. He asked her, "On a starlit night, Alice, have you ever looked up at the sky and wondered who made all this?"

She nodded yes and agreed that he might pray with her. Later that evening she went forward to the mercy seat. Tears of remorse streaming from her eyes, Alice accepted Christ as her Lord and Savior and began a new life leading to increasing serenity. The Spirit of Christ filled the spiritual void that had haunted her for so long.

CALL TO WORSHIP

WE call Salvationists worldwide to worship and proclaim the living God, and to seek in every meeting a vital encounter with the Lord of Life, using relevant cultural forms and languages.

We affirm that God invites us to a meeting in which God is present, God speaks, and God acts. In our meetings we celebrate and experience the promised presence of Christ with his people. Christ crucified, risen and glorified is the focal point, the epicentre of our worship. We offer worship to the Father, through the Son, in the Spirit, in our own words, in acts which engage our whole being: body, soul and mind. We sing the ancient song of creation to its Creator, we sing the new song of the redeemed to their Redeemer. We hear proclaimed the word of redemption, the call to mission and the promise of life in the Spirit.

—Commissioner Robert Street, *Called to be God's People*

Christ Died for a Suffering Alcoholic Like Me

David shared his experience with Jesus in a testimony: "I was caught in the grip of alcohol. It was a compulsion. There was nothing I could do. I thought I was going insane. My life was in rubbles. I had nothing left to stand on. In incredible misery, I really thought I was dying. Gazing at the cross in the ARC chapel, all the things I used to have hints of kind of folded in, and I realized that it was about the death of Christ on the cross!

"I didn't know anything about Christianity. I had never even been in a church before, literally! But I remember the physical, the mental, and the emotional change I felt, and I knew I had been given the gift of sobriety. I left that chapel rejuvenated. I had hope. Later that night during the worship service, I went forward to the penitent form. I knew that Christ had died for a suffering alcoholic like me.

"When God eventually called me to Salvation Army officership, my response was about how I could say 'thank you' to God who had given me such a wonderful gift."

Each one of us is ruled by something. Despite illusions to the contrary, we are never in control of our lives. However, as we make a conscious decision to surrender the care of our will and our lives over to God—to place control where it belongs, in the loving, capable hands of our Creator—we are increasingly set free from the control of our compulsions. *Previously, you let yourselves be slaves to impurity and lawlessness, which led ever deeper into sin. Now you must give yourselves to be slaves to righteous living so that you will become holy* (Rom. 6:19 NLT).

This reminds me of the lyrics of a popular song years ago, "Looking for love in all the wrong places." Many of us have been unknowingly looking for God in all the wrong things and wrong behaviors. When intoxicated, for a while we felt alive and complete, fully self-confident. In his volume *The Addictive Personality*, therapist Craig Nakken explains: "In this trance-like state, the spiritual experience seems real, but is in fact only illusory.... Addiction is a process of buying into false and empty promises."[2]

What we all need is the *real* thing, a vital, authentic encounter with the Lord of Life, Jesus Christ, our *true* Higher Power. The volume *Alco-*

holics Anonymous observes that making progress working the 12 steps can lead to a genuine spiritual connection: "As we felt new power flow in, as we enjoyed peace of mind, as we discovered we could face life successfully, as we became conscious of His presence, we began to lose our fear of today, tomorrow or the hereafter. We were reborn."[3]

Many of us began our walk with Christ at the local Salvation Army ARC. Others of us perhaps accepted Jesus into our hearts elsewhere, but made a serious recommitment to follow him at the chapel altar of the ARC. We found through personal experience that we did not have wisdom enough nor strength enough on our own to live life effectively; we could not stop drinking or using drugs through our own power. We bruised and bloodied ourselves as we repeatedly attempted to break through that brick wall blocking our way to sobriety. We finally gave up and decided to accept God's long-standing offer to help us up from our fallen condition, and we reached out and took his hand.

Step 1
We admitted that we were powerless over drugs and alcohol—that our lives had become unmanageable.

Step 2
[We] came to believe that a Power greater than ourselves could restore us to sanity.

Step 3
[We] made a decision to turn our will and our lives over to the care of God *as we understood him.*

Someone once summarized the first three steps this way: I can't; God can; therefore, I think I'll let Him.

Doctrine 2
We believe that there is only one God, who is infinitely perfect, the Creator, Preserver, and Governor of all things, and who is the only proper object of religious worship.

The fact that there is only one God is declared by Scripture from Genesis to Revelation. God is infinitely perfect in ways our finite minds cannot grasp.

God is the creator of all things. How did the universe, the planet Earth or living things originate? There are those who suggest that lower forms of life "appeared" on the planet, from which all life evolved to higher levels, finally producing man. The variations of this theory are numerous, complex, and changing. However, a careful examination of this theory will show that to believe such a bizarre idea takes far more "faith" than it does to believe the Biblical explanation. Imagine striding through a barren desert and suddenly coming upon a computer lying in the sand. How much "faith" would it take to believe the computer "appeared" as a result of evolution from thin air? It would make far more sense to believe that the computer had an intelligent designer, a creator.

As Preserver and Governor of all things, God rules over that which he has created. He rules over nature. Paul states: *He is before all things, and in him all things hold together* (Col. 1:17). God also rules over human beings, giving them wise and holy laws for their conduct and their physical well-being, rewarding or punishing them, and ruling over all events for the fulfillment of his great purpose. *"The God who made the world and everything in it is the Lord of heaven and earth.... For in Him we live and move and have our being"* (Acts 17:24, 28).

God is the only proper object of religious worship. Our Lord quoted from the Old Testament as a rule of mankind: *"Worship the Lord your God and serve him only"* (Matt. 4:10). Although more than 90% of all Americans admit the existence of God, they don't all worship him. One only truly worships God when he or she surrenders to God. For example, if you sit in a meeting with wickedness, or hatred, in your heart and mind, you are not really worshipping God. The meeting is without meaning to you, and you are not blessed until you make things right with God. The process of making things right with God is the beginning of the journey of recovery.

Doctrine 3
We believe that there are three persons in the Godhead—

the Father, the Son, and the Holy Ghost, undivided in essence and co-equal in power and glory.

There are three persons in the Godhead. While there is only one God, the "essence" that binds the three members of the Trinity together in one is their common nature of deity, of being God. None is less important or subordinate to another. Note, then:

- The Father is God; the Son is God; the Holy Spirit is God.
- We may properly say: God, the Father; God, the Son; God, the Holy Spirit.
- However, the three divine persons are distinct and separate: the Father is not the Son, nor the Holy Spirit; the Son is not the Holy Spirit, nor the Father; the Holy Spirit is not the Father, nor the Son.

The first call stresses: "Christ crucified, risen, and glorified is the focal point, the epicenter of our worship."[4] Who, then, is Jesus Christ?

Doctrine 4
We believe that in the person of Jesus Christ the Divine and human natures are united, so that He is truly and properly God and truly and properly man.

Only God could take away all the sins of all humanity for all time. God became a man, became one of his creations—God incarnate—so that he could share our humanity, then died for us.

God made him who had no sin to be sin for us so that in him we might become the righteousness of God (2 Cor. 5:21). Only *sinless* Jesus could work such a miracle—change places with us, so to speak—so that we too, now no longer stained by sin, could become the temple in which God himself could dwell. Our sins now atoned for by the blood of Christ, his Spirit now indwelling us so we have his mighty weapons at our disposal, we can successfully fight the battle against sin, including addiction. What a miracle!

Doctrine 6
We believe that the Lord Jesus Christ has by His suffering and death made an atonement for the whole world so that whosoever will may be saved.

He is our Savior!

The third person in the Godhead is the Holy Spirit. The first call states: "We offer worship to the Father, through the Son, in the Spirit."[5] Active in convicting the sinner of sin, active in bringing about the spiritual rebirth of each new believer, the role of the Holy Spirit cannot be overstated.

He also has been called the representative of Jesus Christ dwelling within the believer. *You, however, are controlled not by the sinful nature but by the Spirit, if the Spirit of God lives in you. And if anyone does not have the Spirit of Christ, he does not belong to Christ* (Rom. 8:9). The Holy Spirit remains as our ever-present helper. Jesus assures us, *"And surely I am with you always, to the very end of the age"* (Matt. 28:20). The apostle Paul writes to his friends from prison, *for I know that through your prayers and the help given by the Spirit of Jesus Christ, what has happened to me will turn out for my deliverance* (Phil. 1:19).

As believers we gather together frequently to bear one another up as we worship the Lord from the heart. There is something powerful in believers coming together in worship, sharing in a "vital encounter with the Lord of Life."[6]

As an aged disciple, perhaps the last remaining personal witness of the earthly sojourn of Jesus Christ, John wrote: *This is the message we have heard from him and declare to you: God is light; in him there is no darkness at all. If we claim to have fellowship with him and yet walk in the darkness, we lie and do not live out the truth. But if we walk in the light, as he is in the light, we have fellowship with one another, and the blood of Jesus, his Son, purifies us from all sin* (1 John 1:5-7).

Consider the apostle's words: *we have fellowship with one another, and the blood of Jesus, his Son, purifies us from all sins.* Clearly, regular fellowship with other believers is key to maintaining a healthy relationship with Christ. *Let us not give up meeting together, as some are in the habit of doing* warns the writer of the letter to the Hebrews (10:25).

The apostle John reveals to us a vital truth in his account of Jesus' encounter with the woman of Samaria. *"Woman," Jesus replied, "believe me, a time is coming when you will worship the Father neither on this mountain nor in Jerusalem. You Samaritans worship what you do not know; we worship what we do know, for salvation is from the Jews. Yet a time is coming and has now come when the true worshipers will worship the Father in the Spirit and in truth, for they are the kind of worshipers the Father seeks. God is spirit, and his worshipers must worship in the Spirit and in truth"* (John 4:21-24).

Questions to Think About:

1. What does the first call say about the nature of worship?
2. Step four reads: We "made a searching and fearless moral inventory of ourselves." Step five reads: We "admitted to God, to ourselves and to another human being the exact nature of our wrongs." Does working these steps help us to follow the directive to *"worship the Father in the Spirit and in truth"* (John 4:23-24)? Since, according to these Scriptures, God is seeking such worshippers, can we count on him to help us do our moral inventory fearlessly? Does living a present day, obedient, repentant lifestyle help the process? (See 1 John 1:7 and Ephesians 5:25-27.)
3. How can we ensure that we experience a vital personal encounter with Christ in our Salvation meetings?
4. In AA and NA, we often remember that "the newcomer is the most important person." What do we mean by this?
5. Likewise, how relevant is our worship to newcomers? How much would they understand, and what should we do to assist them?

CALL TO GOD'S WORD

WE call Salvationists worldwide to a renewed and relevant proclamation of and close attention to the word of God, and to a quick and steady obedience to the radical demands of the word upon Salvationists personally, and upon our Movement corporately.

We affirm that when the gospel is preached God speaks. The Bible is the written word of God. Preaching is that same word opened, read, proclaimed and explained. When in our human weakness and foolishness we faithfully proclaim and explain the word, the world may hear and see a new thing; God speaks and God acts. To respond in obedient faith results in a decisive encounter with God. We affirm that God speaks profound truth in simple words, common language and potent metaphor, and we confess that at times our words, too often shallow, obscure, archaic or irrelevant, have veiled, not revealed, our God.

—Commissioner Robert Street, *Called to be God's People*

God's Word is living and active and has been written not so that God may see his words in print, but to be obeyed. When the Psalmist wrote, *I have hidden your word in my heart that I might not sin against you* (Ps. 119:11), he was speaking frankly of obedience to God's Word.

As we obey God's instructions, he transforms our will as well as our behavior. Isn't that what we who surrender to God are seeking: for our very will to be modified to comply with God's? The following account shows us this outcome as it was accomplished in the life of an individual.

I Thank God for My Alcoholism

At a recent Alcoholics Anonymous meeting, Jeff shocked the listeners with his opening remark: "I thank God for my alcoholism." You could have heard a pin drop in that room. Every eye was focused on the speaker. He continued: "The reason I say this is because I'm such a pigheaded, obstinate person that if it had not been for the horrendous circumstances—the mess made of my life by my hard-drinking lifestyle—I know that I would never have given my heart to Christ 30 years ago. I thank God for the disease of alcoholism that finally drove me to my knees.

"For years I resisted surrender to him because I knew that if God were in control of my life, then I would not be in control and, therefore, I would not be able to have things the way that I wanted them. I was in such full denial that only a very painful encounter with the consequences of my limitations finally prompted me to make an honest assessment of my life.

"At that point I bent my knees and submitted to God and his total reign in my life. Because of this decision, made out of necessity three decades ago, today I can say sincerely with the apostle Peter in 1 Peter 1:8 that I have been filled with an inexpressible and glorious joy. Therefore, I thank God for my alcoholism."

Doctrine 1
We believe that the Scriptures of the Old and New Testaments were given by inspiration of God and that they only constitute the Divine rule of Christian faith and practice.

There are two major divisions of the Bible, with 39 books in the Old Testament (originally written in Hebrew) and 27 in the New Testament (originally written in Greek). A "testament" is a covenant or an agreement. In the Old Testament, God covenants to provide a redeemer, and in the New Testament, he shows how that covenant was fulfilled in the person of Jesus Christ. Jesus claimed that he was the redeemer promised in the old covenant: *"These are the Scriptures that testify about me,"* he pointed out (John 5:39).

We say of the Scriptures that they "constitute the Divine rule of Christian faith and practice." "Christian faith" refers to our doctrine, or what we believe. For instance, people need to know that they are fallen creatures, sinners by nature and by choice. They need to know that there is a supreme God who created them, loves them, redeemed them through his Son, Jesus, and has planned a glorious eternity for them. God reveals these facts to us in his Word.

"Christian practice" refers to our manner of life and our concept of what is right and wrong. We base our conduct upon the Word of God.

Step 3
[We] made a decision to turn our will and our lives over to the care of God *as we understood him.*

As we in all sincerity make this decision, we are stepping out in faith that there is a God of our own understanding, though he is undetectable through our five senses. If genuine, this is a decisive step of faith. As God catches us up in his strong, loving arms, everything depends on following through with our decision to turn over our will (desires, thinking) and our lives (actions, behavior). As we yield to God the authority to guide our desires, our behavior will follow.

The second call speaks of "a quick and steady obedience to the radical demands of the word."[7] As God guides us, we obey him. Out of love for him we follow him. Our obedience to the Word shows our love for God—it is a natural outcome of our love for him (1 John 4:19). Jesus, the living Word, speaks through the written word: *"Anyone who loves me will obey my teaching. My Father will love them, and we will come to them and make our home with them. Anyone who does not love me will not obey my teaching. These words you hear are not my own; they belong to the Father who sent me. All this I have spoken while still with you. But the Advocate, the Holy Spirit, whom the Father will send in my name, will teach you all things and will remind you of everything I have said to you. Peace I leave with you; my peace I give you. I do not give to you as the world gives. Do not let your hearts be troubled and do not be afraid"* (John 14:23-27).

A decision lacking follow-through is worthless. Likewise the decision to turn our will and lives over to the care of God must be carried out. This starts with step four, where true repentance begins.

Step 4
[We] made a fearless and moral inventory of ourselves.

In step four we list all the significant events—good and bad—in our lives. We do this prayerfully and as honestly as we can. We can confront the most uncomfortable, even frightening, events because we do this step hand in hand with God. *Even though I walk through the valley of the shadow of death, I will fear no evil, for you are with me*, the psalmist prays to our Lord (Ps. 23:4), and so we proceed gingerly, knowing he is with us.

This step is about honesty, with the ultimate goal of uncovering mistaken ways of thinking that are holding us back from a full surrender to our Lord. Once uncovered, with God's help they can be corrected.

Doctrine 7
We believe that repentance towards God, faith in our
Lord Jesus Christ, and regeneration by the Holy Spirit,
are necessary to salvation.

"Repentance" means to turn around, a decision to change that is genuine and reflected by action, sorrow for our sins sufficient enough to lead to obedience. Paul announced, *"I preached that they should repent and turn to God and demonstrate their repentance by their deeds"* (Acts 26:20). Out of love for our Lord, through faith in him, we repent toward God our Father of our willful disobedience, our sins (James 4:17). Relying on

God for the courage and power to follow through with our decision to give up our old sinful lifestyles, we make a decision to change.

However, sometimes the journey to the mercy seat involves a detour. *"Therefore, if you are offering your gift at the altar and there remember that your brother has something against you, leave your gift there in front of the altar. First go and be reconciled to your brother, then come and offer your gift"* (Matt. 5:23-24). Today the gift we bring to the altar is ourselves; *offer your bodies as living sacrifices*, we are urged (Rom. 12:1). But if someone is holding something against us, the Holy Spirit may press us to first get right with that individual.

Step 8
[We] made a list of all persons we had harmed, and became willing to make amends to them all.

We discuss this list with our sponsor. We are careful about whom we ultimately set out to make amends with.

Step 9
[We] made direct amends to such people wherever possible, except when to do so would injure them or others.

Let's say you're setting out to make amends with somebody. You approach the man's house. You ring the door bell. You hear footsteps in the hall. The doorknob turns, and there stands the man you haven't seen in years. A look of full astonishment materializes upon his face.

Nervously you begin, "Derek, I know you're surprised to see me after all this time, but I'm working my 12-step program in AA and I'm on step nine. This step calls for me to make amends with people I have harmed. Well, Derek, you are on my list. Remember what I did to you in June, four years ago? I can see you do remember it! Well, Derek, I would like to make it right with you if I can. Is there anything at all I could do that would make it right with you?"

How Derek responds to this question depends upon a number of things—his personality and the circumstances of the offense, for example.

It may be that his reaction will be one of great relief and a handshake or even a bear hug, accompanied by a comment like: "It's great to see you looking so good after all this time. Let's forgive and forget. It's water under the bridge."

Or Derek may scowl and slam the door in your face! That's certainly possible. But at least you will have the benefit of knowing you did all that you could to mend this particular fence.

However, there may be yet a third reaction: Derek may frown and snap, "Yes, there's something you can do. You can give me $2,000 cash compensation, and we can call it square." Depending upon your circumstances, you may need to work out a payment plan with Derek. But you will soon come to see that it is certainly worth it all in return for ridding yourself of the load of crippling guilt feelings, remorse and shame that now slide comfortably off your shoulders as a result of the simple act of making amends.

You see, working the steps is not so much about the other people in our lives as it is about the recovering person becoming spiritually healthier—getting right with God and oneself, as well as others.

Through God's power, we show both God and others that the change is real. We have joined the ranks of the tens of thousands of human beings who live satisfying, gratifying lives without the use of unprescribed drugs or alcohol. Gone also are all the foolish things we used to do that hurt so many, including ourselves, and broke the heart of God (Eph. 4:30).

The second call reminds us that "at times our words, too often shallow, obscure, archaic or irrelevant, have veiled, not revealed, our God."[8] May we always remember that as regenerated souls, born-again new creations in Christ, we need to step up and prepare ourselves to be effective witnesses. *"We are therefore Christ's ambassadors, as though God were making his appeal through us. We implore you, on Christ's behalf: Be reconciled to God"* (2 Cor. 5:20).

Step 12
Having had a spiritual awakening as the result of these Steps, we tried to carry this message to alcoholics, and to practice these principles in all our affairs.

We learn in Alcoholics Anonymous, "You can't keep it unless you give it away." We keep the sanity God has granted us as we help others who are reaching out for what we now have.

The apostle John expresses very well the practice and rewards of "passing it on": *We proclaim to you what we have seen and heard, so that you also may have fellowship with us. And our fellowship is with the Father and with his Son, Jesus Christ. We write this to make our joy complete* (1 John 1:3-4). The joy we know when we accept Jesus Christ into our hearts is made complete as we proclaim him to others as "the Spirit who inspired the word illumines our hearts and minds."[9]

"If the word of God is to rule our lives, we must study it, heed it—and live by it."[10] This cannot be stressed enough. There is a lot of misunderstanding about this in the church today. While reading, learning and knowing the Word of God is very important, it is only by living it out—by obeying the Word—that we become transformed. It is only through obedience to God's Word that we repent. The 12 steps truly do serve as an avenue through which the Spirit of God transforms us increasingly into his image. Jesus prayed for his disciples, *"Sanctify them by the truth; your word is truth"* (John 17:17).

Questions to Think About:

1. How can we, as an ARC or corps, ensure that we keep the Word of God at the center of our life together?
2. How does "giving away" my sobriety help me keep it? How can the act of "giving away" my faith help me keep it as well?
3. What do you think would happen to Christianity today if the Bible were suddenly taken away? What would we lose? What would we do?
4. How do we follow through with the "decision to turn our will and our lives over to the care of God"?
5. If a person were caught shoplifting, what would he or she have to do to show true repentance?
6. What would you say to a person who emphasizes that to be saved you need "only believe"?

CALL TO THE MERCY SEAT

WE call Salvationists worldwide to recognise the wide understanding of the mercy seat that God has given to the Army; to rejoice that Christ uses this means of grace to confirm his presence; and to ensure that its spiritual benefits are fully explored in every corps and Army centre.

We affirm that the mercy seat in our meetings symbolises God's unremitting call to his people to meet with him. It is not only a place for repentance and forgiveness, but also a place for communion and commitment. Here we may experience a deep awareness of God's abundant grace and claim his boundless salvation. The mercy seat may be used by anyone, at any time, and particularly in Army meetings when, in response to the proclaimed word, all are invited to share loving and humble communion with the Lord.

—Commissioner Robert Street, *Called to be God's People*

The mercy seat (also called the penitent form) is the bench or table provided as a place where people can kneel to pray, seeking salvation or sanctification, or making a special consecration of their life to God's will and service. This piece (or combination) of furniture is usually located between the platform and the main area of Army halls in much the same way as other Christian churches place altars, as a focal point to remind worshippers of God's reconciling, redeeming presence. It symbolizes God's continuing call to his people to meet with him. Although the mercy seat does not posses any spiritual power of its own, nevertheless, kneeling at the mercy seat can mean a great deal to the repenting person.

Commissioner Street observes, "The act of kneeling shows humility, dying to self and submission to God. The act of standing after an encounter with God can also symbolize being raised to new life." He quotes Commissioner Phil Needham, "The true mercy seat is of the heart, and the outward act of kneeling at a prayer bench, or any other place, is nothing if not the outward sign of a kneeling soul."[11]

Serving at ARCs for over 20 years, I have spotted many a beneficiary or ARC alumnus slip into an otherwise empty ARC chapel and kneel silently at its mercy seat. Likewise, I have observed many a saved soul begin their journey with the Lord by kneeling at the mercy seat following an altar call. I have seen many step seven prayers—"humbly asked God to remove our shortcomings"— confirmed at the mercy seat. There is something about the willful action of getting up from the pew, walking down the aisle, and kneeling at the mercy seat in front of both God and man that helps the brand new believer respond in truth to the conviction of the Holy Spirit.

Kneeling is the outward demonstration of the inward act of resisting Satan's lure and humbling oneself before God. *But he gives us more grace. That is why Scripture says: "God opposes the proud but gives grace to the humble." Submit yourselves then to God. Resist the devil, and he will flee from you. Come near to God and he will come near to you* (James 4:6-8).

Surrendering False Pride

Getting down on your knees for the first time at the mercy seat can be a very humbling experience for an addict. If it's done in all sincerity, then it's an admission that God is greater. An alcoholic has been called "an egomaniac with an inferiority complex." False pride is one of the first things that has to go if one is to succeed in recovery.

Bill had a lot of false pride. At his first meeting with his ARC chaplain, he blurted out, "I want you to know that I have an IQ of 165!"

"And how is that working for you?" replied the chaplain.

At their meeting the following week, Bill entered with a lowered head and a sunken demeanor. In his hand he bore a letter from his wife detailing what she called his "offenses." "I've read this over at least five or six times," he said sheepishly. "It's damp with my tears. I had no idea she saw me this way or even that I had done half the things she says I did—I was drinking, you know. Reading it has been very humbling. It has knocked the stuffing right out of me. For the first time since I arrived here I've been wanting a drink."

The chaplain gently guided Bill toward the alternative—to accept Christ as Lord and Savior and rely on him rather than the alcohol he had turned to in the past. The chaplain explained that Christ is the true answer, not a counterfeit substitute. In Christ lies true peace of mind; alcohol leads only to chaos and emotional turmoil. When the chaplain shared with him John the Baptist's words, *"He must become greater; I must become less"* (John 3:30), Bill smiled meekly. "I get it," he said. "I need to get out of his way and let God take control." Bill left the office in a thoughtful mood.

During the altar call in that evening's chapel service, Bill was among the first to approach the mercy seat. As the chaplain placed a hand on his shoulder and offered to lead him in the prayer of salvation, Bill nodded and whispered, "He must become greater; I must become less." Accepting Christ, he prayed, "Dear God, help me to be humble and remain that way. Help me to remember that I am only a man, and I need your help to stay sober, one day at a time."

Doctrine 6
We believe that the Lord Jesus Christ has by his suffering and death made an atonement for the whole world so that whosoever will may be saved.

Atonement has been described in this way: Our sinful lifestyles (our willful disobedience of God's commands) once separated us from God, who made us for himself in the first place. Since God is a God of justice, someone had to pay for our sins if we were ever to be reunited with him. God chose to be that individual, to pay the price himself. Atonement has been loosely defined as "at-one-ment"—the union of the exalted and resurrected Lord with you and me, his creation. We are now one, praise God! God redeemed us himself; he paid the price. The cross bridges the gulf, the chasm, separating earth and heaven. Atonement is the redeeming effect of Christ's incarnation (becoming a man), his sufferings (on the cross), and his death. Therefore, the cross of Christ is at the center of the atonement.

Paul expressed it this way: *What a wretched man I am! Who will rescue me from this body of death? Thanks be to God—through Jesus Christ our Lord.... [T]hrough Jesus Christ the law of the Spirit of life set me free from the law of sin and death* (Rom. 7:24-8:2). "*He will save his people from their sins,*" the angel told Joseph (Matt 1:21). Jesus is called *Immanuel—which means "God with us*" (v. 23). For this salvation to be ours, however, there is something we must exert: our will. We each have a choice.

This exertion of the will may start the journey of repentance—a response to conviction by the Holy Spirit that results in a change of attitude, of behavior, of lifestyle. Paul teaches: *Godly sorrow brings repentance that leads to salvation and leaves no regret, but worldly sorrow brings death* (2 Cor. 7:10). "Rarely have we seen a person fail who has thoroughly followed our path," state the authors of *Alcoholics Anonymous*.[12] The "path" to which they are referring is, of course, the journey of the 12-step program, a series of Biblical mandates succinctly laid out—which may be equated to the process of repentance—and which include following through with our decision to surrender to the will of God (step three).

This journey of repentance—letting go and letting God take over control of our lives as we invite him to guide us in self-examination (step four) and confession (step five)—takes particular depth in step six.

Step 6
[We] were entirely ready to have God remove all these defects of character.

In this step, we consider what many of us had failed to consider before, that drinking or using drugs may only be a symptom of something deeper that is troubling us. And while we may be willing to surrender to God some of these deeper defects of character, we may struggle with giving them all over to him. We find it hard to understand that giving up drinking or using drugs means giving over all of our defects of character. But if Christ is to dwell within this temple that is ourselves, he wants to make it all over new. Our body is his new home, and God will not dwell within anything that is stained by sin. *Do you not know that your body is a temple of the Holy Spirit, who is in you, whom you have received from God? You are not your own; you were bought at a price. Therefore honor God with you body* (1 Cor. 6:19-20).

Questions to Think About:

1. In what way does the mercy seat serve as a place of humble communion with the Lord? How does the act of kneeling show humility?
2. What role can kneeling at the mercy seat play in the step three "decision to turn our will and lives over to the care of God"?
3. How can the mercy seat serve as a place for repentance and forgiveness?
4. Some people do not accept the divinity of Christ. What effect would that have on the atonement?

CALL TO CELEBRATE
CHRIST'S PRESENCE

WE call Salvationists worldwide to rejoice in our freedom to celebrate Christ's real presence at all our meals and in all our meetings, and to seize the opportunity to explore in our life together the significance of the simple meals shared by Jesus and his friends and by the first Christians.

We affirm that the Lord Jesus Christ is the one true sacrament of God. His incarnation and continuing gracious presence with his people by means of the indwelling Holy Spirit is the mystery at the heart of our faith. We hear our Lord's command to remember his broken body and his outpoured blood as in our families and in our faith communities we eat and drink together. We affirm that our meals and love feasts are an anticipation of the feasts of eternity, and a participation in that fellowship which is the Body of Christ on earth.

—Commissioner Robert Street, *Called to be God's People*

And he took bread, gave thanks and broke it, and gave it to them, saying, "This is my body given for you; do this in remembrance of me" (Luke 22:19). Jesus was sharing a Jewish custom when he was recorded as saying, *"Do this."* He was in a home, not a church. He was at a meal table, not a communion rail. He did not say communion could only be administered by ordained priests or ministers. It is evident that Jesus did not inaugurate here a new sacramental ritual. He first declared that the Passover supper, which was of the old covenant, was but a symbol of His own death which would seal the new covenant. In the Passover the Jews served unleavened bread and a cup of wine. So Jesus declared prophetically: *"This [the bread] is my body given for you…. This cup is the new covenant in my blood, which is poured out for you"* (Luke 22:19-20). Paul explained later: *Christ, our Passover lamb, has been sacrificed* (1 Cor. 5:7). Jesus gave us a directive to remember his death whenever we eat or drink: *"Do this in remembrance of me."* We do this when we ask the blessing before eating.

Paul presented the same principle to the Corinthians of remembering the Savior's death at church meals (1 Cor. 11:33), which had come to be called *"the Lord's Supper"* (v. 20). But church history bears out that during the first century, when the New Testament was written, there was no "Lord's Supper" in the form of a sacramental church observance. This sacramental observance was a development of the second or third century.

Jesus Christ is the one true sacrament of God. *The Word became flesh and made his dwelling among us,* declares the apostle (John 1:14). Further, Jesus promises: *"Where two or three come together in my name, there am I with them"* (Matt. 18:20).

Because you are his sons, God sent the Spirit of his Son into our hearts, the Spirit who calls out, "Abba, Father," Paul says (Gal. 4:6). Elsewhere, he explains: *God has chosen to make known among the Gentiles the glorious riches of this mystery, which is Christ in you, the hope of glory. We proclaim him…. To this end I labor, struggling with all his energy, which so powerfully works in me* (Col. 1:27-29). Christ's Spirit is ever within us to strengthen us, teach us and guide us. *Those who are led by the Spirit of God are sons of God,* stresses Paul (Rom. 8:14). Jesus is within all who are saved. Jesus is among us when we gather in his name.

How Can God Accept a Man like Me?

Like a terrifying scene from a horror movie, Jimmy descriptively related each detail of the explosion of his meth lab five years before:

the screams of pain from his best friend, the wailing sound of the approaching sirens, the demanding yells of his partner: "We've got to get out of here! The police are on their way. We've got to go now! Now!" Climbing into the car with his partner, Jimmy looked over his shoulder one more time at the smoking building. That last glance at his best friend was emblazoned upon his mind: the gasping sobs, the burning body, the face twisted in pain.

Recounting the real life nightmare, Jimmy squirmed in his chair, his voice breaking as the tears soaked the handkerchief in his hands. "See what I did! My lifelong friend died. I did not stay with him. I ran away! To save my own hide! Instead of staying with him, helping him! How can God ever accept a man like me? A man with blood on his hands!"

The ARC chaplain shared with Jimmy the welcome news that none of us can earn our own salvation. Both the murderer and the gossiper stand on level footing—all are equally unfit for God. *It is by grace you have been saved, through faith—and this is not from yourselves, it is the gift of God—not by works, so that no one can boast* (Eph. 2:8-9). Through a marvelous act God became one of his own creations— he became a human, the man Jesus Christ. Then, in a miraculous exchange while he hung on the cross, Christ switched places with us. Our sins were placed in him and his righteousness was placed in us. Jesus took the punishment we deserved so we might be made right with him. Through his resurrection we now have the opportunity for a new, eternal, *"rich and satisfying life"* (John 10:10 NLT).

Therefore, the chaplain was able to tell Jimmy that God had not only forgiven him but had even forgotten the bad things Jimmy had done. Not even the horrifying incident at the meth lab five years before would separate him from the love of God. As the chaplain prayed the prayer of salvation with Jimmy, the Spirit of Christ entered into him, set up residence in his life and started him on a brand new adventure. Jimmy came to know the peace of God through the indwelling Holy Spirit. This is the presence of Christ we celebrate at our meals together.

Doctrine 8
We believe that we are justified by grace through faith in
our Lord Jesus Christ and that he that believeth hath
the witness in himself.

"Justification" has been defined loosely as "just as if I had not sinned."
So it is that once we are saved our past sins are both forgiven and
forgotten by our God. All those horrid, haunting deeds we committed
when still practicing our addiction are no longer counted in the sight of
God.

Through faith in Jesus Christ we are made right with our Creator,
so the divine union with him is now possible and genuine. Grace is the
undeserved favor of our Lord. It is mercy outpoured. He sets us free of
the "wreckage of our past." Now he helps us move on.

Step 3
[We] made a decision to turn our will and our lives over
to the care of God *as we understood Him.*

Once I've made a genuine decision to surrender all control of my
will and my life to my Lord—and followed through with it—then I am
content, for I am his. I no longer walk alone. I know this through the
witness of the Spirit of Christ within me, God's own testimony. "He
that believeth hath the witness in himself." Taken directly from 1 John
5:10 (KJV), this statement tells us that we may know that we are saved.
It has been described as that quiet, assured feeling when we are safe in
the house during a violent blizzard outside. We are sheltered and secure.
The apostle John elaborates: *And this is how we know that he lives in us:
We know it by the Spirit he gave us* (1 John 3:24).

Commissioner Street reminds us: "The preaching of the cross was
at the centre of the apostle Paul's ministry (1 Corinthians 1:23). It must
always be at the heart of the Army's life and worship."[13] Christ incarnate
walked among us; Christ crucified, resurrected, and now in Spirit lives

within us and is in our midst, guiding and empowering us. Without him, we cannot succeed in maintaining our walk of recovery; however, with him we cannot fail.

May we rely on his power consistently and thereby not fall. In our simple meals together, as well as in our wider fellowship meals, may we always pray and remind ourselves: Christ is within us; Christ is in our midst.

Questions to Think About:

1. How does Christ indwelling us make all the difference to us in our journey of recovery from addiction to drugs and alcohol?
2. What is the importance of acknowledging Christ as being in our midst at our meals and meetings?
3. God loves all people very much. Then why could he not forgive people their sins without his Son having to die on the cross? Was Christ's death really necessary?
4. What do we mean by improving "our conscious contact with God" (step 11)?
5. You know you are an American if you were born in the USA. You know you are alive because it hurts when you are pinched. How do you know that you are a Christian?
6. How well do you understand and live out the truth of "Christ in me"?

CALL TO SOLDIERSHIP

WE call Salvationists worldwide to recognise that the swearing in of soldiers is a public witness to Christ's command to make disciples and that soldiership demands ongoing radical obedience.

We affirm that Jesus Christ still calls men and women to take up their cross and follow him. This wholehearted and absolute acceptance of Christ as Lord is a costly discipleship. We hear our Lord's command to make disciples, baptising them in the name of the Father, the Son and the Holy Spirit. We believe that soldiership is discipleship and that the public swearing-in of a soldier of The Salvation Army beneath the Army's Trinitarian flag fulfils this command.

It is a public response and witness to the life-changing encounter with Christ which has already taken place, as is the believers' water baptism practised by some other Christians.

—Commissioner Robert Street, *Called to be God's People*

A Man Who Beat the Odds

"People used to tell me, 'You're rushing toward death.' The things I did in my addiction shame me today," Stan confesses. "Now I apply that same energy toward my brand new life."

After catching his first prison term at age 18, prison became a "revolving door" for him, Stan says. By age 55, he had spent altogether 35 years behind bars. "I never allowed myself to stay out long enough to learn to take life on life's terms. Then three years ago, God showed me I can have a better way of life with him," Stan declares.

"Walking the prison yard in Chino those last days, I thought a lot," he adds. "There weren't many options for somebody like me—someone who had spent his whole life in prison. 'What are my odds?' I asked myself. But I made a commitment that somehow, some way, I was going to stay clean."

When he accepted Christ at the ARC chapel altar, for the first time in his life Stan felt clean inside. This rejuvenated him. God laid a burden for helping others on him, and at the same time he learned that belonging to a church family was essential to recovery. "I used to be a soldier in the bad sense: I talked tough when the cells were locked. But now I felt compelled to serve as a soldier in the good sense, engaged in spiritual warfare through The Salvation Army. But if the drugs were my right hand, the cigarettes were my left."

After a major internal spiritual battle, Stan laid down not only the drugs and alcohol but a lifelong cigarette habit as well. It wasn't long before he was commissioned as a local officer for the corps. Yet he is an avid Narcotics Anonymous 12-stepper as well. Today Stan assists in leading a weekly NA meeting at the ARC and sponsors many of the men. "I have to stay busy in my recovery," he insists, "because I want to keep this victory that eluded me for so long. I'm on a downward-going escalator. I may be facing the right direction, trying to do the right thing, but if I'm not taking positive steps forward in my recovery, that escalator is going to take me down. I used to be all in for my addiction, but today I'm all in for God."

Once we are saved, indwelled by the empowering Holy Spirit, it makes sense that soldiership should follow. As Paul tells his mentee, Timothy, *Endure hardship with us like a good soldier of Christ Jesus* (2 Tim. 2:3).

When Jesus said, *"If anyone would come after me, he must deny himself and take up his cross and follow me"* (Matt. 16:24), his hearers couldn't miss the imagery. The cross was the Roman method of execution. Jesus was telling would-be disciples, "If you're going to follow me, assume the attitude of a condemned criminal and be ready to die." Over the centuries since, many disciples of Christ followed his directions all the way to martyrdom. Our new life in Christ comes with a cost. We determine to deny our selfish desires and follow Christ's leading, whatever it may entail. It takes courage, but if we rely on him, Jesus never lets us down.

The commission affirms that "Jesus Christ still calls men and women to take up their cross and follow him. This wholehearted and absolute acceptance of Christ as Lord is a costly discipleship."[14] Soldiership is discipleship. How costly it is may vary from person to person and culture to culture. However, if it isn't costly, it isn't real discipleship, for discipleship always entails obedience to the Lord's commands.

Doctrine 9
We believe that continuance in a state of salvation depends upon continued obedient faith in Christ.

Commissioner Street points out, "The swearing-in ceremony. . . is a means whereby a new soldier professes new life in Christ. . . . It is inconceivable that a disciple would promise to follow Jesus and not expect to continue to obey the Master. . . . So discipleship for a soldier includes the promise to be responsive to the Holy Spirit's promptings and obedient to his leading. . . . It includes the intention to grow in grace through worship, prayer, service and the study of Scripture. There is the promise to make the values of the Kingdom of God and not the values of the world the standard of life."[15]

No one recognizes the need and urgency of these basic principles more than the recovering drug addict or alcoholic. It is a given that without ongoing responsiveness to the directions of the 12-step program, a person will not remain clean and sober. Continuing to work the program is the medicine we take to keep in check our chronic disease of drug or alcohol addiction. Many of us have discovered this the hard way—by falling flat on our face more than once after allowing ourselves to deviate from the teachings of the program. Steps 10, 11 and 12 provide us with clear-cut directions on how to maintain our sobriety.

Step 10
[We] continued to take personal inventory and when we were wrong promptly admitted it.

The daily discipline required to do this step is one of the keys to long-term recovery; strict obedience is necessary. It must be an ongoing process. To skip even a day may mean death to our sobriety. The recovering person may be victimized by his or her own emotions as dishonesty, selfishness, resentment or fear—of which God had cleansed him or her during the prior steps—crop up once more, reclaiming ownership of the mind and soul. Paul gives us fair warning: *Do not let the sun go down while you are still angry and do not give the devil a foothold* (Eph. 4:26-27). It's essential to nip these destructive tendencies in the bud while they are still incipient—before they lead to the desire to drink or use. Strict obedience as a good soldier of Jesus Christ is required.

Paying close attention to and carefully relying on God, not only for direction but also for inspiration and strength, is so very crucial. We discover that none of us can be obedient to God without his help. We are truly clean and sober one day at a time as we rely on him one step at a time.

In our ninth doctrine we are also saying that we believe it is possible for those who have been truly converted to fall away and be eternally lost. The Christian is saved through faith, which includes commitment. That same faith which was necessary to be saved is also necessary to keep salvation. It is required that such faith be a continuing commitment—a day-by-day experience. Note that in John 3:16 the expression *believes in* is in the present tense; it's a continued process, not just a "once-for-all" act of faith.

The Greek word "pisteuo," which is translated "believes in" in John 3:16 and multiple other places in Scripture, means literally "trusts in, clings to, or relies on." It is not what you believe about Jesus that leads to salvation, but rather the practice of continually "relying on" him. One might correctly paraphrase John 3:16 as follows: *For God so loved the world that he gave his one and only Son, that whoever believes in [trusts in, clings to, relies on] him shall not perish but have eternal life.* We are saved from our sins—from our compulsions to drink alcohol or use drugs, from giving in to various disobedient compulsions in all their forms—as we continue to trust in, cling to, and rely on Jesus as our Higher Power. As we faithfully do this, he empowers us to remain obedient.

This is frequently stated in the Bible. Take, for example, John 5:24, *"I tell you the truth, whoever hears my word and believes him who sent me has eternal life."* In this case both "hear" and "believe" are in the present tense. If you put them into the past tense—"heard," "believed," and you "had" eternal life—you cancel the great benefit of eternal life.

The Scriptures agree that continuance in a state of salvation depends upon continued obedient faith in Christ. You wouldn't expect it to be otherwise. It's true everywhere. If you are going to be safe in the jungle, stay with your guide. If you are going to be safe on the highways, obey the traffic laws. If you are going to be safe in the water, don't rock the boat. If you are going to be safe (saved) as a Christian, keep your commitment to your Savior.

Assurance is given that we need not backslide. When we are tempted to sin—to do something we know God doesn't approve of—if the Spirit of God indwells us, he will not allow the temptation to be more than we can stand; he will provide a way out (1 Cor. 10:13).

However, we have the responsibility to watch and pray that we will not give in to temptation (Matt. 26:41) and to grow and mature in the Lord (2 Peter 3:18), to become a *workman … who correctly handles the word of truth* (2 Tim. 2:15). Then it can be said with Peter, *For if you do these things, you will never fall* (2 Peter 1:10).

Questions to Think About:

1. What happens to us at the moment of conversion?
2. Why do you think it is that God doesn't keep all his children so that they are not *able* to fall away and be lost eternally?

3. In what ways can we ensure that our obedience to the ongoing call of discipleship is maintained?
4. What do you think would lead a person to appear to work a good recovery program for perhaps a number of years, then slack off on the "maintenance steps" of 10 through 12, ultimately relapsing?

CALL TO THE INNER LIFE

WE call Salvationists worldwide to enter the new millennium with a renewal of faithful, disciplined and persistent prayer; to study God's word consistently and to seek God's will earnestly; to deny self and to live a lifestyle of simplicity in a spirit of trust and thankfulness.

We affirm that the consistent cultivation of the inner life is essential for our faith life and for our fighting fitness. The disciplines of the inner life include solitude, prayer and meditation, study, and self-denial. Practising solitude, spending time alone with God, we discover the importance of silence, learn to listen to God, and discover our true selves. Praying, we engage in a unique dialogue that encompasses adoration and confession, petition and intercession. As we meditate we attend to God's transforming word. As we study we train our minds toward Christlikeness, allowing the word of God to shape our thinking. Practicing self-denial, we focus on God and grow in spiritual perception. We expose how our appetites can control us, and draw closer in experience, empathy and action to those who live with deprivation and scarcity.

—Commissioner Robert Street, *Called to be God's People*

Commissioner Street reminds us: "The disciplines of the inner life, when applied, help us discover what God wants to give us and make us. They can draw us closer to him, make us more aware of him and improve our perspective on life."[16] As the "Call to Salvationists" reminds us: "The vitality of our spiritual life as a Movement will be seen and tested in our turning to the world in evangelism and service, but the springs of our spiritual life are to be found in our turning to God in worship, in the disciplines of life in the Spirit, and in the study of God's word."[17]

Paul coaxed the church in Philippi: *Therefore, my dear friends, as you have always obeyed—not only in my presence, but now much more in my absence—continue to work out your salvation with fear and trembling, for it is God who works in you to will and to act according to his good purpose* (Phil. 2:12-13). Someone once summarized this passage this way: God "works in" what we "work out."

Obedience to God's program is one of the requirements for spiritual growth. Wonderfully, God not only asks us to live a godly life but also provides us with the power to accomplish it. He works in us, giving us the desire and the ability to obey him. As we get to know him better through Bible study and spending time with him in prayer, he transforms us from the inside out so that we can shine brightly for him. The apostle is reminding the Philippians to continue in singleness of purpose with active reverence towards God, maintained through practicing the activities that enhance spiritual growth and maturation.

Step 11

[We] sought through prayer and meditation to improve
our conscious contact with God, *as we understood
Him*, praying only for knowledge of His will for us and
the power to carry that out.

Both "The Call to the Inner Life" and step 11 advise us to carry out daily spiritual maintenance. The Bible and other devotional Christian literature—as well as prayer and meditation and self-denial (fasting from food or drink or other substances)—serve as key tools for lasting Christian growth. In step 11 we slow down, take ourselves out of the driver's seat, and set aside a specific time to seek God's will through prayer and meditation on his Word.

The "Call to the Inner Life" emphasizes, "Practising solitude, spending time alone with God, we discover the importance of silence, learn to listen to

God, and discover our true selves. Praying, we engage in a unique dialogue that encompasses adoration and confession, petition and intercession. As we meditate we attend to God's transforming word."[18]

Steps four through seven have been called the supernatural steps, a working out of the prayer found in Psalm 139:23-24: *Search me, O God, and know my heart. Test me and know my anxious thoughts. See if there is any offensive way in me and lead me in the way everlasting.* As God looks within us and shows us the naked truth about ourselves, he also gives us the courage to confess our newfound realizations to him, to ourselves, and to one another. As he guides us along his approved way to live, he discards our defects of character, transforming us from the inside out.

Don't Let the Sun Go Down on Your Anger

Ronnie had two years in recovery, he said, when one evening as he was praying, seeking God's help in self-examination, his eyes popped open in surprise, then expanded in horror at a sudden revelation: "Oh, no! I'm building a resentment toward Tommy at work! Come to think of it, he's been badmouthing me all over the work place. I think he's after my job! In fact, I almost took his head off in the passageway the other day! Oh, no! This is going to get me drunk. If I let the sun go down on this anger, it will most assuredly give the devil a foothold."

Following the instructions he had learned from AA, he said, "I got on my knees and asked God to please take the resentment away! I pleaded and pleaded with him. Then I called my sponsor, who I had on speed dial." Ronnie informed his sponsor, "God has just revealed to me that I'm developing a strong resentment toward a coworker. You know what that means!" Ronnie quoted from the AA book: "Resentment is the number one offender; it destroys more alcoholics than anything else."[19]

"Can we meet over coffee and pie?" he asked his sponsor, adding, "I'll buy. I need to unload, to vent about this until the resentment fades." That evening, Ronnie met with his sponsor at a restaurant and talked all evening. Eventually Ronnie felt better, but the resentment was still nagging at him.

On the way home he stopped and attended a meeting. He had learned from AA that being of service is one of the best ways to let go of anger. He also knew that the Bible advises us to reach out with a helping hand to others. Jesus taught that a true disciple of Christ should be a servant of all (Matt. 10:42). Glancing around the meeting hall, Ronnie spotted a newcomer, trembling and teary-eyed, who looked as if he had not bathed in a week. Though he didn't feel like striking up a conversation with him, Ronnie, following the nudging of the Spirit, walked over and introduced himself. The newcomer smiled weakly. "Would you like to talk?" Ronnie asked him.

"Can I?" was the response. Like a geyser, the newcomer unloaded—the words gushing forth from him. Ronnie listened patiently as the young man shared about his difficulties with his wife, his work and the law. He was so glad to find a listening ear that Ronnie felt good to be there for him. All he had to do was listen and offer a few encouraging words.

Driving home that night, Ronnie marveled at the difference between the newcomer and himself. "Compared to his problems," Ronnie said to himself, "my own difficulties are quite small." Suddenly he realized that his resentment toward his coworker had been lifted. It was completely gone! "Thank you, Lord!" he exclaimed out loud. "Thank you for setting me free. I won't be drinking today!" The following morning he made amends with his coworker, as he knew he should. God's Word, as seen through the lens of AA, is a marvelous tool for sustaining recovery. It works if you work it.

Step 7
[We] humbly asked Him to remove our shortcomings.

This step requires the utmost of humility. We need humility so that we can recognize the severity of our character defects; so that we can acknowledge the limits of human power in addressing these character defects; and so that we can appreciate the enormity of God's power to transform our lives. The invitation to humility is not an invitation to low self-esteem or a negative self-image; in fact, the opposite is true. Healthy self-esteem frees us to receive and appreciate God's greatness as we turn over to him our broken, defective personalities so that he may mold them into effective instruments of his will. AA's seventh step prayer words this commitment as follows: "My Creator, I am now willing that you should have all of me, good and bad. I pray that you now remove from me every single defect of character which stands in the way of my usefulness to you and my fellows. Grant me strength, as I go out from here, to do your bidding. Amen."[20]

Doctrine 7
We believe that repentance towards God, faith in our Lord Jesus Christ, and regeneration by the Holy Spirit, are necessary to salvation.

Doctrine 9
We believe that continuance in a state of salvation depends upon continued obedient faith in Christ.

A question I hear often from new Christians is this: "I love the Lord, and I've accepted Jesus Christ as my Lord and Savior. But sometimes I still sin. So what do I do?" The apostle John gives us this advice: *My dear friends, I write this to you so that you will not sin. But if anybody does sin, we have one who speaks to the Father in our defense—Jesus Christ, the Righteous One. He is the atoning sacrifice for our sins, and not only for ours but also for the sins of the whole world* (1 John 2:1-2). He goes on to say, *We know that we have come to know him if we obey his commands* (1 John 2:3).

The message here: Stay close to Christ. Consistently cultivate a strong Christ-centered inner life through study of God's Word and prayer. Maintain a consistent, quality devotional life. If we live like this, but still stumble by committing a sin, we react like the persistent cowboy who, though thrown from his horse, promptly gets up, dusts himself off, and gets back into the saddle again. He does not give up. In other words, if we sin, God convicts us; consequently, we immediately repent, ask God's forgiveness, and determine that, with the Holy Spirit's help, we will not repeat the sin but live obediently. As we mature spiritually, we find ourselves sinning less and less frequently.

John declares: *The reason the Son of God appeared was to destroy the devil's work. No one who is born of God will continue to sin, because God's seed remains in him; he cannot go on sinning, because he has been born of God* (1 John 3:8-9).

Questions to Think About:

1. How can we ensure that our prayer life is given priority each day?
2. How can keeping a consistent devotional life help prevent us from relapsing on drugs or alcohol?
3. What is the evidence of genuine repentance?
4. In what ways can we ensure that faithful, disciplined and persistent prayer is at the heart of our corps life?

CALL TO OUR LIFE TOGETHER

WE call Salvationists worldwide to rejoice in their unique fellowship; to be open to support, guidance, nurture, affirmation and challenge from each other as members together of the body of Christ; and to participate actively and regularly in the life, membership and mission of a particular corps.

We affirm the unique fellowship of Salvationists worldwide. Our unity in the Holy Spirit is characterized by our shared vision, mission and joyful service. In our life together we share responsibility for one another's spiritual well-being. The vitality of our spiritual life is also enhanced by our accountability to one another, and when we practise the discipline of accountability our spiritual vision becomes objective, our decisions more balanced, and we gain the wisdom of the fellowship and the means to clarify and test our own thinking. Such spiritual direction may be provided effectively through a group or by an individual. Mutual accountability also provides the opportunity to confess failure or sin and receive the assurance of forgiveness and hope in Christ.

—Commissioner Robert Street, *Called to be God's People*

The commission calls Salvationists everywhere to affirm one another, to be there for each other. When Jesus was speaking to his disciples shortly before his crucifixion, he informed them, *"By this all men will know that you are my disciples, if you love one another"* (John 13:35). So Christ's words ring out to us across the centuries. As a part of the body of Christ, Salvationists are held to the same standard. Jesus directs us: *"Do to others as you would have them do to you"* (Luke 6:31). It's only as we love one another that people recognize us as Christians. In Scripture, love is an action word, not a warm fuzzy feeling; it is manifested in our behavior toward one another.

Hand in Hand to Salvation

The young man, heavily tattooed on both his face and arms, was new to the ARC program. From his chair he glanced down at the floor hesitantly, then turned back to the chaplain expectantly. "I don't believe in God. But I want to," he announced. "Can you show me how to believe that God exists?"

As the chaplain took Richard gently on a journey through Scripture, then showed him how to pray, Richard shared that his entire dorm had been praying for him. "They want me to find what they have, and I want it, too!" he said, explaining that he wanted to "feel" God. The chaplain shared with him that there is a significant difference between a chemically induced feeling—as he was accustomed to with drugs and alcohol—and the spiritual awareness of God's presence. At that, Richard glanced quizzically about and replied that he did not want to accept Christ right now but would think hard on what he had been told. Richard departed the office in a very contemplative mood.

At 4 p.m., the receptionist phoned. "Chaplain, Richard's here to see you."

Richard entered, followed by two others, all of them grinning from ear to ear. "You're Richard's dorm mates, aren't you?" the chaplain asked.

"Yes," they replied. Tim and Ed had been in the program three months already and had accepted Christ early on. All three men appeared so very excited that the chaplain began to get excited, too! He sensed that something wonderful was coming, and he waited.

Richard broke the ice. "Chaplain," he said, "I've been thinking hard about our talk this morning, and I've decided to accept the Lord today!

Today! And if it's alright with you, I asked my friends to be here, too."

"Praise the Lord!" the chaplain exclaimed. "Tim and Ed, I think it's wonderful that you are here with Richard on this special occasion. Faith is a walk that we always take with others. We never walk it alone."

He invited the little band to form a circle. As they clasped hands together, emotionally he prayed: "Our blessed Lord and Savior, we bring to you our brother, who's surrendering to you his heart and life and will."

Following his lead, solemnly Richard prayed:

"Lord Jesus, how I love you, how I need you!
I open up my heart to receive you.
Thank you, Lord, for dying on the cross for my sins,
For pardoning my wrongs. Set me completely free
Of the bondage of myself—I've been so in love with me!
Show me how each day I may best serve Thee;
Make me into the man you want me to be."

As they congratulated their brother, they sensed another presence, a band of angels with them, a celestial chorus. The excited young men departed, slapping each other on the back. Alone in his office, the chaplain tearfully knelt and prayed: "Thank you, Lord, for the gift of your sweet grace today."

The 12-step program is a social program as well as a spiritual one. You may notice that the 12 steps never begin with the word "I." The first word in step one is "we." In other words, recovery can only be done in community; the road to recovery is not meant to be traveled alone. As the commission states: "In our life together we share responsibility for one another's spiritual well-being…. Mutual accountability also provides the opportunity to confess failure or sin and receive the assurance of forgiveness and hope in Christ."[21]

Step five is the spiritual exercise of confession:

Step 5

[We] admitted to God, to ourselves, and to another
human being the exact nature of our wrongs.

Commissioner Street speaks of the value of "mentoring or using a
spiritual director to assist with spiritual development." Such a person,
he advises, should be "possessed by the Spirit," a person of experience
and discernment who knows how to "give way to the Holy Spirit."[22] In
AA and NA, a sponsor is someone of the same gender who has lengthy
sobriety—a minimum of one year, but the more sobriety the better.
He or she has worked all 12 steps—or is at least two steps ahead of the
sponsee—and makes the commitment to meet weekly with the sponsee,
coaching him or her along the 12-step journey. Today there are many
advanced in AA or NA to whom a new person in recovery may turn for
direction in working the 12 steps. You recognize your sponsor as one
who has been where you are and therefore knows what you are going
through, and one who has what you are seeking: sobriety—victory over
addiction.

Fellow Salvationists who are also brothers and sisters in recovery
from drugs and alcohol bring something special to the sponsor-spon-
see relationship. Such accountability partners can keep us focused
on our recovery in Christ. Ecclesiastes 4:9-12 tells us: *Two are better
than one, because they have a good return for their work: If one falls down,
his friend can help him up. But pity the man who falls and has no one to
help him up!... Though one may be overpowered, two can defend themselves.*
Proverbs 27:17 points out, *As iron sharpens iron, so a friend sharpens a
friend* (NLT).

If your sponsor is not a mature Christian, you might also consider
developing a relationship with someone who is competent to guide
you in your spiritual growth. This person should also have a strong
personal recovery program, or at least be knowledgeable about drug
and alcohol recovery. Without this knowledge base, some well-mean-
ing Christian pastors or lay leaders may inadvertently mislead the recovering person. James advises us *confess your sins to each other and pray
for each other so that you may be healed. The prayer of a righteous man is*

powerful and effective (James 5:16). A sponsor or accountability partner who is also a prayer partner is invaluable.

Questions to Think About:

1. How committed are we to one another in Christlike love?
2. In what way is our walk of recovery equivalent to our walk of faith with Christ?
3. What advantage do you see in having a sponsor who can also serve as a prayer partner?
4. How can fellowship with other Salvationists play a significant role in our recovery?
5. Does active participation in a home corps strengthen a person's recovery program? Should it replace working a 12-step program (as some choose)?

CALL TO OUR LIFE IN THE WORLD

WE call Salvationists worldwide to commit themselves and their gifts to the salvation of the world, and to embrace servanthood, expressing it through the joy of self-giving and the discipline of Christlike living.

We affirm that commitment to Christ requires the offering of our lives in simplicity, submission and service. Practising simplicity we become people whose witness to the world is expressed by the values we live by, as well as by the message we proclaim. This leads to service which is a self-giving for the salvation and healing of a hurting world, as well as a prophetic witness in the face of social injustice.

—Commissioner Robert Street, *Called to be God's People*

Doctrine 5

We believe that our first parents were created in a state of innocency, but by their disobedience they lost their purity and happiness, and that in consequence of their fall all men have become sinners, totally depraved, and as such are justly exposed to the wrath of God.

A rich man once said, "I'm nothing special. Like many others, I'm just a sinner saved by grace." Standing in one of the poorer cities of the world, looking about him at the poverty of the landscape, he added, "There but for the grace of God go I."

This illustration and the Biblical principles expressed in doctrine five remind us that we are all on similar footing. Without Christ suffering and dying for us, we would all be in desperate straits: "sinners, totally depraved," we are all "justly exposed to the wrath of God." *Yet while we were still sinners, Christ died for us* (Rom. 5:8). Christ didn't wait for us to straighten up, clean up and get our act together; otherwise none of us would make it to heaven. *We love because he first loved us* (1 John 4:19).

Saying "Thank You" to God

Ted had recently accepted Christ and was seeking in some small way to repay the Lord for not only saving his soul but delivering him from the desire to drink and use drugs. He described his dilemma this way: "I turned in all sincerity to God and laid this question before him: 'Lord, you have done so much for me! Thank you for saving my life! Now I deeply desire to do something for you in return. What can I do to express the extent of my deep appreciation to you?'"

The Lord told him: "Be content with your life, be considerate of others in everything you do, and continue to love me with all your heart."

"Of course I will, Lord," Ted replied. "I will always love and praise you; I cannot help but do so, for you have saved my life! But I want to do even more!" Then Ted said that the words of an old hymn he had heard as a child popped into his head: "He's got the whole world in his hands!" And instantly he knew there was nothing more he could give God. He had given Jesus the right to himself, the one thing God had allowed him to retain. But he craved to do still more. Then in his reading one day, he came upon these words of Christ in Matthew: "*Come, you who have won my Father's blessing! Take your inheritance—the kingdom reserved for you since the foundation of the world! For I was hungry and you gave me food. I was thirsty and you gave me a drink. I was a stranger and you made me welcome. I was naked and you clothed me. I was ill and you came and looked after me. I was in prison and you came to see me there…. I assure you that whatever you did for the humblest of my brothers you did for me*" (Matt. 25:34-36, 40 J.B. Phillips).

"The words leaped off the page at me!" he explained. "They hit home—an epiphany that set my heart dancing." And he understood that he should give his thanks offering to God by helping hurting people. This would be his new purpose for living.

When asked how she could daily work patiently among the dead and dying of Calcutta, Mother Teresa quoted Christ's words, "Whatever you do for one of the least of these, you do for me." Consequently, she said, she saw the face of Jesus in the face of each sick and dying person she helped. May we do likewise!

Step 12 elucidates the spiritual principle of servanthood, which is not only the key to long-term recovery but to strengthening our faith walk as well; there is really no difference for the Christian in recovery.

Step 12
Having had a spiritual awakening as the result of these Steps, we tried to carry this message to alcoholics, and to practice these principles in all our affairs.

The spiritual awakening is a very powerful event in the lives of recovering people, as we come to an awareness that God has dramatically transformed our lives, bringing us the serenity and peace that we craved for so long. We cannot help but want to share the message with others that their lives are not hopeless after all. They too can have what we have found!

Doctrine 6
We believe that the Lord Jesus Christ has by His suffering and death made an atonement for the whole world so that whosoever will may be saved.

Through showing we love one another, we spread the good news of the gospel. Scripture says whosoever will may be saved (John 3:16) therefore, if others will listen to us, we attempt to show them the way. If whosoever will may be saved, then it is important that people be given a choice; together as a body of Christ we can bring that message to many.

Paul spells it out clearly: *"Everyone who calls on the name of the Lord will be saved." How, then, can they call on the one they have not believed in? And how can they believe in the one of whom they have not heard? And how can they hear without someone preaching to them? And how can they preach unless they are sent? As it is written, "How beautiful are the feet of those who bring good news!"* (Rom. 10:13-15).

When General Gowans presented The Salvation Army mission slogan, "Save souls, grow saints and serve suffering humanity," he was laying out three integrally related elements. As we Salvationists express our love of the Lord Jesus by reaching out indiscriminately to serve suffering humanity in his name, the other commands follow. We "saints" are strengthened in our faith as we share it; souls are saved as the result of being touched by the love of Jesus; the faith walks of others are strengthened as "saints" work alongside them in ministry. It is a very beautiful thing.

Questions to Think About:

1. How does the awareness of the extent of Jesus Christ's suffering for us lead us to follow in his steps?
2. To what extent is self-giving and Christlike living evident in our fellowship today?
3. In what ways can you offer more of your life in simplicity, submission and service?
4. How can God make us more what we should be?
5. Why do you think God makes it necessary for people to "will" or want to be saved before they can be saved?

CALL TO CULTIVATE FAITH

WE call Salvationists worldwide to explore new ways to recruit and train people who are both spiritually mature and educationally competent; to develop learning programmes and events that are biblically informed, culturally relevant, and educationally sound; and to create learning environments which encourage exploration, creativity and diversity.

We affirm that our mission demands the formation of a soldiery who are maturing, and are being equipped for faithful life and ministry in the world. In strategic and supportive partnership with the family, the Christian community has a duty to provide opportunities for growth into maturity by means of preaching and teaching, through worship and fellowship, and by healing and helping.

—Commissioner Robert Street, *Called to be God's People*

In the ninth call, the commission calls us to go further and identify people who are spiritually mature and educationally competent, and to encourage them to put their gifts to good use serving Christ. There are a number of powerful Scripture verses addressing spiritual maturity. Here are three:

Brothers, stop thinking like children. In regard to evil be infants, but in your thinking be adults (1 Cor. 14:20).

When I was a child, I talked like a child, I thought like
a child, I reasoned like a child. When I became a man,
I put childish ways behind me (1 Cor. 13:11).

Prepare God's people for works of service, so that the body
of Christ may be built up until we all reach unity in the
faith and in the knowledge of the Son of God and become
mature, attaining to the whole measure of the fullness
of Christ. Then we will no longer be infants, tossed back
and forth by the waves, and blown here and there by
every wind of teaching and by the cunning and craftiness
of men in their deceitful scheming (Eph. 4:12-14).

The message of the ninth call, cultivating faith, is "the formation of
a soldiery who are maturing and being equipped for a faithful life and
ministry in the world."[23] As we mature in recovery, we reach out to
replace ourselves, to bring others along the path we are traveling. "Faith
is not static. It must develop to stay alive…. It ceases to be faith unless
it is applied," writes Commissioner Street.[24] "The spiritual life is not a
theory. We have to live it," reads *Alcoholics Anonymous*.[25] *Do not merely*
listen to the word, and so deceive yourselves. Do what it says (James 1:22).

Commissioner Street stresses the importance of the devotional life
for spiritual growth for the teacher, who then passes it on to the pupil:
"Quiet times, study of the word of God, consistent openness to learning more about our great God and his ways, are essential to spiritual
development," he writes.[26] *Alcoholics Anonymous* stresses similar tactics
for recovery.

Step 10
[We] continued to take personal inventory and when we
were wrong promptly admitted it.

"We have entered the world of the Spirit. Our next function is to
grow in understanding and effectiveness…. It is easy to let up on the
spiritual program of action and rest on our laurels [our past accomplish-

ments]. We are headed for trouble if we do, for alcohol is a subtle foe. We are not cured of alcoholism. What we really have is a daily reprieve contingent on the maintenance of our spiritual condition."[27] You can't make it any clearer than that. If each of us in recovery will take heed of this warning, we will not fail. The message is quite clear: continue cultivating faith. God is working in us—"we have entered the world of the Spirit"—now let us not "let up on the spiritual program of action."

Living Oneself into Right Thinking

"She's right, you know! I am a dirty dog! I am a worm! All the names she calls me, they're true! I'm not sure I even want to live anymore!" Mark was having a hard time facing the consequences of his past sinful lifestyle—using and selling drugs for almost 20 years. Clean and sober now for a few weeks, the tremendous toll the lifestyle had taken on his wife and children was finally hitting home. He had made the momentous decision of accepting Christ and had asked Jesus to forgive him. What remained now was the necessary task of forgiving himself.

Remorse can be crippling, tripping us up into relapse and backsliding; continuously reliving the past can become a rehearsal for the future. We are advised in Colossians 3:13, *Bear with each other and forgive whatever grievances you may have against one another.* The Greek pronoun translated "one another" emphasizes the fact that we are all members of Christ's body—everyone members one of another—so that in forgiving each other we also forgive ourselves. However, knowledge of this truth alone is insufficient. How does a person live it out?

It was Chuck C. who observed in his remarkable book, *A New Pair of Glasses*, "You can live yourself into right thinking, but you cannot think yourself into right living."[28] The founders of AA hit on something wonderful when they discovered the power of working an action program. The secret of successful recovery is the *action* element; we make progress in healthy thinking only through actively participating in our program. Consequently, the only way Mark could ever let go of self-hatred and resentment—which if left untended would invariably lead him back to his old lifestyle—was to go to work on his personal program of recovery.

The chaplain guided Mark into behaving in a forgiving manner toward others in the program and in his personal life. When we pray for our enemies, it changes us on the inside. Jesus, of course, knew this, when he instructed, *"Pray for those who persecute you"* (Matt. 5:44). When Mark was angry and judging others, he was in the chaplain's office often, seeking direction on how to actively forgive and pray for them. As he learned through practice how to forgive others, eventually he had to forgive himself. The path of forgiveness inevitably leads us back home, for we cannot truly forgive others unless we first forgive ourselves. Once Mark arrived there, like the apostle Paul, he could only move forward: *Forgetting what is behind and straining toward what is ahead, I press on toward the goal to win the prize for which God has called me heavenward in Christ Jesus* (Phil. 3:13-14).

Mark's salvation eventually led him to inner peace, but this did not occur until he put his newfound faith to work. He eventually lived himself into right thinking.

Doctrine 9
We believe that continuance in a state of salvation depends upon continued obedient faith in Christ.

Faith must include obedience in order for it to be a saving faith. As a matter of fact, in every reference to "faith" in the Bible as a means of salvation, the saving faith is an obedient faith. Saving faith is more than believing—it involves a commitment to what we believe. *But someone will say, "You have faith; I have deeds." Show me your faith without deeds, and I will show you my faith by what I do. You believe that there is one God. Good! Even the demons believe that—and shudder. You foolish man, do you want evidence that faith without deeds is useless?* (James 2:18-20). Without the works springing from our faith, our faith really is a dead thing—it will eventually die in our hearts.

Questions to Think About:

1. We read *faith by itself, if it is not accompanied by action, is dead* (James 2:17). What is James' meaning?
2. We are reminded that victorious living depends upon continued obedient faith in Christ. How does obedience to the commands of the gospel strengthen and keep alive our Christian faith?
3. What does the spiritual maturity we seek involve?
4. What initiatives should be introduced to enhance the cultural relevance of our Salvation Army programs and mission?

CALL TO HOLINESS

WE call Salvationists worldwide to restate and live out the doctrine of holiness in all its dimensions—personal, relational, social and political—in the context of our cultures and in the idioms of our day while allowing for, and indeed prizing, such diversity of experience and expression as is in accord with the Scriptures.

We affirm that God continues to desire and to command that his people be holy. For this Christ died, for this Christ rose again, for this the Spirit was given. We therefore determine to claim as God's gracious gift that holiness which is ours in Christ. We confess that at times we have failed to realise the practical consequences of the call to holiness within our relationships, within our communities and within our Movement. We resolve to make every effort to embrace holiness of life, knowing that this is only possible by means of the power of the Holy Spirit producing his fruit in us.

—Commissioner Robert Street, *Called to be God's People*

Doctrine 5
We believe that our first parents were created in a state of innocency, but by their disobedience they lost their purity and happiness; and that in consequence of their fall all men have become sinners, totally depraved, and

as such are justly exposed to the wrath of God.

Because of their disobedience, not only did Adam and Eve become sinners, but all their descendants as well. Paul declares in Romans 3:23, for all have sinned and fall short of the glory of God, and reiterates in Romans 5:12, sin entered the world through one man, and death through sin, and in this way death came to all men, because all sinned. Because the perfect man of creation was marred by his disobedience, all people are born with a natural bent, or tendency, to sin. This is called "depravity." The doctrine of holiness presents the necessity of not only being forgiven of our sins, but also of being cleansed from our sinful nature.

Doctrine 10
We believe that it is the privilege of all believers to be wholly sanctified, and that their whole spirit and soul and body may be preserved blameless unto the coming of our Lord Jesus Christ.

Sanctification is understood as the process by which believers are increasingly transformed by the Holy Spirit into the image of Christ. The standard for all Christians is to be like Christ—and that is holiness. The Bible tells us that the only way to true Godlikeness, true holiness, is by becoming entirely or wholly sanctified. *May God himself, the God of peace, sanctify you through and through. May your whole spirit, soul and body be kept blameless at the coming of our Lord Jesus Christ. The one who calls you is faithful and he will do it* (1 Thess. 5:23-24).

In the heart of the sincere believer there is often a struggle, a cruel struggle, against evil. The Bible shows that we do not need to continue this struggle between the ruling principle of God, which we received when we were saved, and the ruling principle of sin—the sinful nature—which we inherited from Adam. Speaking of the ruling principle as a law, Paul says, *through Christ Jesus the law of the Spirit of life set me free from the law of sin and death* (Rom. 8:2). This deliverance from our inherited tendency to sin is termed the experience of "entire sanctification."

Commissioner Street explains that people or things only become holy when they participate in the life of God. *His divine power has given us everything we need for life and godliness through our knowledge of him who calls us by his own glory and goodness. Through these he has given us his very great and precious promises, so that through them you may participate in the divine nature and escape the corruption in the world caused by evil desires* (2 Peter 1:3-4). The action we take as Christians, as we follow Biblical mandates, leads to the accomplishment of this goal, if we choose to make it our goal. The continuation of this passage from Peter makes this clear: *For this very reason, make every effort to add to your faith goodness; and to goodness, knowledge; and to knowledge, self-control; and to self-control, perseverance; and to perseverance, godliness; and to godliness, brotherly kindness; and to brotherly kindness, love. For if you possess these qualities in increasing measure, they will keep you from being ineffective and unproductive in your knowledge of our Lord Jesus Christ* (v. 5-8). Peter goes on to imply that this journey of increasing spiritual maturation, resulting from participation in the divine nature, should be the journey of every Christian. *But if anyone does not have them, he is nearsighted and blind, and has forgotten that he has been cleansed from his past sins*, he states emphatically (v. 9).

Anyone looking carefully at steps 10, 11 and 12 of the 12-step program can see the progress of a journey toward holiness:

Step 10
[We] continued to take personal inventory and when we were wrong promptly admitted it.

Step 11
[We] sought through prayer and meditation to improve our conscious contact with God, *as we understood Him*, praying only for knowledge of His will for us and the power to carry that out.

Step 12
Having had a spiritual awakening as the result of these Steps, we tried to carry this message to alcoholics, and to practice these principles in all our affairs.

In its explanation of steps 10 and 11—the journey toward improving "our conscious contact with God"—*Alcoholics Anonymous* stresses the importance of continued effort and action in this way: "Much has already been said about receiving strength, inspiration, and direction from Him who has all knowledge and power. If we have carefully followed directions, we have begun to sense the flow of His Spirit into us. To some extent we have become God-conscious. We have begun to develop this vital sixth sense. But we must go further and that means more action."[29]

"The experience of holiness isn't merely a very blessed spiritual feeling on a Sunday morning," stresses Commissioner Street. "If it is anything at all, it has its outworking in everyday life, seven days a week. Holiness demands that we get our hands dirty while asking God to keep our hearts clean. It must make a defining difference as to how we live and to the people we are."[30]

A Beacon of God's Light

Arthur and his younger sister suffered as they grew up watching their parents drink and use drugs. "I felt a deep emptiness inside," he remembers. "Any attention was always negative. It was, 'Go up to your room! It's adult time,' so they could get loaded." Addicted early on to marijuana and methamphetamine, by age 18 Arthur was breaking into homes and stealing cars to fund his addiction. The behaviors led to jail and homelessness. But everything changed when, at age 24, he accepted Christ at the ARC altar. "I asked him, 'God, now that you've shown me love, please let me know your plan for me. What do you want me to do?'" God's response was clear: "Arthur, I'm taking you out of your comfort zone. Trust me and be still." From that moment forward everything was new and different—and, oh, so rewarding!

Just 18 months later, Arthur was attending college studying to be a nurse. He was also a Salvation Army soldier and a 12-step sponsor with a youth Sunday school and men's ministry, a post he held for years. "I tell my students and mentees, 'I was right where you are. But you don't have to go through what I did. There's a far better way to find the love and compassionate attention you seek.' God pulled me out of the muck and mire and placed me on the rock of salvation to show others the way. I no longer feel a spiritual void—like there's a piece of me missing. As long as I continue to do what I'm doing, I feel complete. I feel happiness. God led me to The Salvation Army for a divine purpose: to be a beacon of God's light. I tell others who are lost like I once was: 'Follow Jesus! He's the true light!'"

Commissioner Street quotes Commissioner Phil Needham: "The holiness of God invites us to look honestly at our lives, to see where transformation is needed, and by his sanctifying grace actually to make those changes."[31] Likewise, *Alcoholics Anonymous* reminds us that we simply cannot recover unless we examine ourselves with meticulous honesty: "Those who do not recover are people who cannot or will not completely give themselves to this simple program, usually men and women who are constitutionally incapable of being honest with themselves."[32] The commission looks to Salvationists to "resolve to make every effort to embrace holiness of life, knowing that this is only possible by means of the power of the Holy Spirit producing his fruit in us."[33]

Galatians 5:22-23 informs us that the fruit of the Holy Spirit is *love, joy, peace, patience, kindness, goodness, faithfulness, gentleness, and self-control.* Just as the fruit of a plant is not manifested immediately upon the seed being sown, so the fruit of the Holy Spirit is generally cultivated over time as the Christian matures spiritually. We Salvationists believe "it is the privilege of all believers to be wholly sanctified." Therefore, says the commission, we "determine to claim as God's gracious gift that holiness which is ours in Christ."[34]

Commissioner Street reminds us that "the apostle Paul urges his fellow-Christians to offer their bodies as living sacrifices 'holy and pleasing to God' (Rom. 12:1). He warns against conforming to the pattern of the world and urges transformation by allowing God to renew our thinking.… There is no sitting on the fence, no compromise. 'Do not be overcome by evil, but overcome evil with good' (v. 21). Be holy!"[35]

Questions to Think About:

1. In what ways does being descendants of Adam make it necessary for us to not only be forgiven of our sins, but also to be delivered of a sinful nature?
2. How can sanctification help us not to backslide, or relapse, in our addictions?
3. What makes God's people holy?
4. What are the personal practical implications of embracing holiness of life?

CALL TO WAR

WE call Salvationists worldwide to join spiritual battle on the grounds of a sober reading of Scripture, a conviction of the triumph of Christ, the inviolable freedom and dignity of persons, and a commitment to the redemption of the world in all its dimensions—physical, spiritual, social, economic and political.

We affirm that Christ our Lord calls us to join him in holy war against evil in all its forms and against every power that stands against the reign of God. We fight in the power of the Spirit in the assurance of ultimate and absolute victory through Christ's redemptive work. We reject extreme attitudes towards the demonic: on the one hand, denial; on the other, obsession. We affirm that the body of Christ is equipped for warfare and service through the gifts of the Spirit. By these we are strengthened and empowered. We heed the injunction of Scripture to value all God's gifts, and rejoice in their diversity.

—Commissioner Robert Street, *Called to be God's People*

Commissioner Street reminds us: "The Salvation Army was born to battle. From its earliest days war on evil was declared. One month before The Christian Mission became The Salvation Army,

William Booth spoke to a War Congress: 'We are sent to war,' he said. 'We are not sent to minister to a congregation and be content if we keep things going. We are sent to make war ... and to stop short of nothing but the subjugation of the world to the sway of the Lord Jesus.'"[36]

As the commission stated, a serious, "sober reading of Scripture" makes it clear that we must "join spiritual battle."[37] The notion is by no means exaggerated. Scripture is rife with references to spiritual warfare. Here is a sample:

> *But I see another law at work in the members of my body, waging war against the law of my mind and making me a prisoner of the law of sin at work within my members* (Rom. 7:23).

> *The weapons we fight with are not the weapons of the world. On the contrary, they have divine power to demolish strongholds* (2 Cor. 10:4).

> *For our struggle is not against flesh and blood, but against the rulers, against the authorities, against the powers of this dark world and against the spiritual forces of evil in the heavenly realms* (Eph. 6:12).

Doctrine 1
We believe that the Scriptures of the Old and New Testaments were given by inspiration of God, and that they only constitute the Divine rule of Christian faith and practice.

All Scripture is God-breathed (2 Tim. 3:16) and constitutes God's "rule of Christian faith and practice." Christian practice refers to our manner of life and our concept of what is right and wrong. And we proceed accordingly. The Salvation Army believes that God calls us to enjoin in a battle *against the spiritual forces of evil in the heavenly realms* (Eph. 6:12).

The picture of a Christian as a soldier is one of the most vivid metaphors in the New Testament. Imprisoned in Rome for a second time, facing imminent death at the hand of the insane emperor Nero, the battle-weary apostle Paul wrote a final letter to his young friend Timothy. Knowing the struggles his young protégé was facing, Paul encouraged him: *Endure hardship … like a good soldier of Christ Jesus. No one serving as a soldier gets involved in civilian affairs—he wants to please his commanding officer* (2 Tim. 2:3-4). Modern-day Christians are still enlisted by *the Captain of their salvation* (Heb. 2:10 KJV) to fight the forces of darkness.

Each piece of the spiritual armor in Ephesians 6:13-17 except the sword is defensive in nature. As recovering addicts, we need to continually improve our conscious contact with God, to know him better, and to surround ourselves with truth, righteousness, faith and prayer. These protect us against the assault of hostile spiritual forces. Arrayed with other Christian soldiers, God gives us weapons that are adequate for our defense. Part of that armor—the shoes—enables us to share the good news of God's delivering power with others, giving hope to them while strengthening our own recovery.

Doctrine 11
We believe in the immortality of the soul; in the resurrection of the body; in the general judgment at the end of the world; in the eternal happiness of the righteous, and in the endless punishment of the wicked.

One of the factors that drives our salvation mission is the truth that the soul will not cease to exist. All believers will have a new spiritual body (1 Cor. 15:44), yet God *"has set a day when he will judge the world with justice"* (Acts 17:31). Hell is the place, or state, of final punishment for the wicked who die in their sins (Matt. 25:33-34, 41). For the sake of those who otherwise may be lost, we must not hesitate to spread the message that it is never too late. "Whosoever will" may still be saved (John 3:16 KJV).

Step 12
Having had a spiritual awakening as the result of these
steps, we tried to carry this message to alcoholics, and
to practice these principles in all our affairs.

Considering that there are numerous Scriptures supporting each
of the 12 steps, we can state unequivocally that as we obey Christ by
working the steps, we grow stronger and stronger spiritually, improving the quality of our recovery. In other words, recovery is both
maintained and strengthened as we practice the powerful step 12,
which incorporates "practicing these principles [working the steps]
in all our affairs."

A key element in recovery is the recognition that we are engaged
in spiritual warfare. "[W]e have been not only mentally and physically ill, we have been spiritually sick. When the spiritual malady is
overcome, we straighten out mentally and physically."[38] But it is not
enough to simply surrender; now we must press on, actively and obediently following our Captain's orders. If we do not do so, we lose
all we have gained: "We trust infinite God, not our finite selves."[39]
Following our Captain's orders, we plunge into action, with an ever
continuing sense of urgency. As our self-seeking character slips away,
"we will suddenly realize that God is doing for us what we could not
do for ourselves."[40] This is the famous "spiritual awakening."

A Higher "Higher Power"

The uniformed Salvation Army soldier gestured dramatically toward the brown paper bag on the floor at his feet. Turning to the ARC
congregation, he remarked, "In talking with some of you earlier in the
lobby, you indicated you don't believe in a Higher Power." Reaching
deliberately into the bag, he retrieved a large brown bottle shaped pre-
cisely like a container of alcohol. As he placed it upon the lectern, a gasp
went up from the congregation. Every single eye in the room was fixed
upon the large brown bottle.

Stepping back, the speaker pointed a finger directly at the bottle. *"That's* a higher power," he announced, "and it had me by the nose for 15 years—until I found a higher 'Higher Power' in the Lord Jesus Christ. Praise him!"

Just as *Alcoholics Anonymous* calls alcohol a "subtle foe," Scripture calls Satan a schemer (2 Cor. 2:11) who attempts to deceive us as he *masquerades as an angel of light* (2 Cor. 11:14). Therefore, although we may be firmly grounded in sound doctrine, we need to constantly be aware of the fierce, invisible warfare that Satan wages against us. Many of our struggles with addiction could be the result of direct attacks by spiritual enemies. We need to constantly be reminded of our inability to manage our lives on our own and to constantly, consciously allow God to stand with us in our battle.

Whether Satan tempts us to relapse in recovery or kicks us when we are already down, we are commanded to be careful and stand firm against him. Meeting with others in recovery will help us see that victory over addiction is attainable and that we are not alone in the battle. Commissioner Street pointedly reminds us that while Biblical reference after reference directs us to have "an appropriate fear of the Lord ... nowhere in Scripture are we told to fear the devil."[41]

On the contrary, he emphasizes, "In James 4:7 we are urged to 'resist the devil' with the promise that he will then flee from us.... Although we must not be careless, flippant, unguarded or foolishly dismissive of the devil, we need never fear him."[42] We are reminded it is only with God's help that we can resist him as he tempts us to relapse in our recovery, backsliding in our faith. Satan is an intimidating foe.

Yet, "we reject extreme attitudes toward the demonic," reports the commission, "on the one hand denial; on the other obsession."[43] Paul declares unequivocally: *For I am convinced that neither death nor life, neither angels nor demons, neither the present nor the future, nor any powers, neither height nor depth, nor anything else in all creation, will ever be able to separate us from the love of God that is in Christ Jesus our Lord* (Rom. 8:38-39).

Questions to Think About:

1. What important difference is there between a divine rule of faith and a divine rule of practice?
2. What do we mean by the term "spiritual warfare"? How important is it that we as Salvationists be engaged in spiritual battle?
3. How committed are we to fighting evil in all its forms?
4. What kinds of resources from the Holy Spirit do we need to draw on to be effective for Christ?
5. How do we guard ourselves against "extreme attitudes toward the demonic"?

The Twelfth Call

CALL TO THE FAMILY

WE call Salvationists worldwide to restore the family to its central position in passing on the faith, to generate resources to help parents grow together in faithful love and to lead their children into wholeness, with hearts on fire for God and his mission.

We affirm that the family plays a central role in passing on the faith. We also recognise that families everywhere are subject to dysfunction and disintegration in an increasingly urbanised world in which depersonalisation, insignificance, loneliness and alienation are widespread. We believe that in the home where Christ's Lordship is acknowledged, and the family is trained in God's word, a spiritually enriching and strengthening environment is provided.

—Commissioner Robert Street, *Called to be God's People*

It becomes clear in recovery that restoration of the family requires faithfulness to working the program over time. This is a powerful effort, with enormous potential not only for the immediate family but for all society. The family, a key unit in society, is ultimately responsible for passing on the faith to its individual members, and to the surrounding community. Fidelity and commitment from both husband and wife is the key to the survival of the family.

One of the most practical, useful truths revealed to us through recovery is that genuine love is not simply a warm, fuzzy feeling (despite the message to the contrary of numerous pop songs, movies, and novels). Until this particular epiphany hits us, we are only spinning our wheels. God's Word teaches that love is always a very active thing. Love for God is obedience (John 14:23-24), while love for others is depicted as acts of service, as in the parable of the good Samaritan (Luke 10:25-37).

As we grasp this and learn to live it out in our relationships with God and others (particularly within our individual families), a whole new world opens before us. However, discovering and incorporating this basic principle into our lives takes work.

Love is an Action Word

One day Erik burst into the ARC chaplain's office hopping mad. "I can't believe my family! I just can't believe them! I've told them a hundred times what they need to do in order for me to stay sober. But nothing's changed at home! Nothing!"

Erik was scheduled to complete the six-month residential program in the ceremony that evening and return home. But he had just discovered that the stressors of home life that had contributed to his drinking problem were still in place. He felt that his father, who was residing with him and his wife, was still inappropriately bossing him around; his wife, Rosa, who was a heavy drinker also, was still drinking in his presence. Other relatives comprised the household as well—his mother-in-law and two grandchildren; a small crowd lived in this home. Erik had determined that before he would move back, there had to be some changes—some order, some serenity—in the house. Otherwise, he was not going home right away.

After the ceremony, when he informed his wife of the decision, she lit into him. "I can't believe you're doing this to me!" she shouted.

Erik responded, "I've told you again and again. Nothing's changed at home. If I go home now, I know I'll soon be drinking again. And I want to stay sober. If you love me, you will make the changes at home that you need to make. I can't come home until then. One thing I've learned well: True love is not just words alone—it is action!"

Steaming, Rosa drove home that night reflecting on her husband's words. "Can what Erik said be true?" she asked herself. By the time she pulled into her driveway, she had concluded that her husband was right. That night she called all the members of the family together and spelled it out to them: Erik was not coming home until certain changes were made.

After leveling with the other members of the household, Rosa had to confront herself. Sitting alone at the dining room table, she gazed at the drink in front of her. The thought of drinking less scared her. But there was another option: she could quit altogether. That thought terrified her. Then it suddenly occurred to her: was it possible that she was an alcoholic like Erik? They had first met over alcohol. Their early dates—in fact their whole life for years—had revolved around alcohol. Erik had given up drinking. Should she?

Now Rosa turned to Jesus for help. She had surrendered her heart to Christ in a midweek chapel service at the ARC, not long after her husband did. Now with all her heart she asked God for direction and for the help to be obedient to his guidance. After she prayed, she knew she should stop drinking.

Three weeks later Erik came home to an orderly family—with no alcohol in the house. As a result of love in action, for God and for one another, the family grew stronger; God had his way.

"'The family ... has enormous potential, including that of life itself, and it is not surprising that, when it becomes disordered, it possesses an equal potential for terrible destruction.' These words of psychiatrist-scholar Dr. Robin Skynner remind us that to ignore the family and its needs is to invite trouble," notes Commissioner Street.[44]

If our family ties are strengthened in our recovery, we can have a powerful positive impact on the families of those around us. The Salvation Army has always promoted the value of family, not only in our worship services, but in our social programs to youth and to the fundamental family unit, as well as in our programs for the elderly.

Commissioner Street also reminds us of the central place in our family lives of "grace at meal times, family prayers, shared worship on Sundays and a social life based within a Christian fellowship."[45]

Involving our children in corps youth programs is crucial if they are to find stability in an increasingly urbanized world where, as Commissioner Street points out, "depersonalisation, insignificance, loneliness and alienation have become widespread."[46] The ancient teaching, *Train a child in the way he should go, and when he is old he will not turn from it* (Prov. 22:6), still applies. Examples abound which illustrate that even if a child ultimately does deviate from the Christian walk, he or she is far more likely to return to it if exposed to the faith as a child.

Doctrine 2
We believe that there is only one God, who is
infinitely perfect, the Creator, Preserver, and Governor
of all things, and who is the only proper object of
religious worship.

As society degenerates and people turn to the false gods of wealth, power, intoxicating substances, and so on, individuals are increasingly alienated. Through the family life, families talking to each other and passing sacred truths through the generations, souls are led home to the true God. For only he is the "proper object of religious worship." Only he will fill the spiritual void in the heart of every human being. The only social remedy for the world remains a spiritual one—and the duty to communicate that truth falls to every Salvationist, to every Christian.

Questions to Think About:

1. In what ways do we give quality time to the essential needs (physical and spiritual) of our families? What can we do better?
2. How can having an abusive parent make it difficult for someone to trust God? How can we help such a person overcome this stumbling block?

3. What are some of the "false gods" worshiped in society today? How do these "false gods" let people down?
4. How can families be helped through our corps to experience faithful love and holy living?
5. In what unique ways can Christian families reach out to hurting families they encounter?

APPENDIX A
The 12 Steps of Alcoholics Anonymous

1. We admitted we were powerless over alcohol—that our lives had become unmanageable.
2. Came to believe that a Power greater than ourselves could restore us to sanity.
3. Made a decision to turn our will and our lives over to the care of God *as we understood Him*.
4. Made a searching and fearless moral inventory of ourselves.
5. Admitted to God, to ourselves, and to another human being the exact nature of our wrongs.
6. Were entirely ready to have God remove all these defects of character.
7. Humbly asked Him to remove our shortcomings.
8. Made a list of all persons we had harmed, and became willing to make amends to them all.
9. Made direct amends to such people wherever possible, except when to do so would injure them or others.
10. Continued to take personal inventory and when we were wrong promptly admitted it.
11. Sought through prayer and meditation to improve our conscious contact with God, *as we understood Him*, praying only for knowledge of His will for us and the power to carry that out.

12. Having had a spiritual awakening as the result of these Steps, we tried to carry this message to alcoholics, and to practice these principles in all our affairs.

APPENDIX B

The Doctrines of The Salvation Army

1. We believe that the Scriptures of the Old and New Testaments were given by inspiration of God and that they only constitute the Divine rule of Christian faith and practice.
2. We believe that there is only one God, who is infinitely perfect, the Creator, Preserver, and Governor of all things, and who is the only proper object of religious worship.
3. We believe that there are three persons in the Godhead—the Father, the Son and the Holy Ghost, undivided in essence and co-equal in power and glory.
4. We believe that in the person of Jesus Christ the Divine and human natures are united, so that He is truly and properly God and truly and properly man.
5. We believe that our first parents were created in a state of innocence, but by their disobedience they lost their purity and happiness, and that in consequence of their fall all men have become sinners, totally depraved, and as such are justly exposed to the wrath of God.
6. We believe that the Lord Jesus Christ has by His suffering and death made an atonement for the whole world so that whosoever will may be saved.
7. We believe that repentance towards God, faith in our Lord Jesus

Christ, and regeneration by the Holy Spirit, are necessary to salvation.

8. We believe that we are justified by grace through faith in our Lord Jesus Christ and that he that believeth hath the witness in himself.

9. We believe that continuance in a state of salvation depends upon continued obedient faith in Christ.

10. We believe that it is the privilege of all believers to be wholly sanctified, and that their whole spirit and soul and body may be preserved blameless unto the coming of our Lord Jesus Christ.

11. We believe in the immortality of the soul; in the resurrection of the body; in the general judgment at the end of the world; in the eternal happiness of the righteous; and in the endless punishment of the wicked.

APPENDIX C
Articles Of War for Salvation Army Soldiers

HAVING accepted Jesus Christ as my Saviour and Lord, and desiring to fulfil my membership of His Church on earth as a soldier of The Salvation Army, I now by God's grace enter into a sacred covenant.

I believe and will live by the truths of the word of God expressed in The Salvation Army's eleven articles of faith:

We believe that the Scriptures of the Old and New Testaments were given by inspiration of God and that they only constitute the Divine rule of Christian faith and practice.

We believe that there is only one God, who is infinitely perfect, the Creator, Preserver, and Governor of all things, and who is the only proper object of religious worship.

We believe that there are three persons in the Godhead—the Father, the Son and the Holy Ghost—undivided in essence and coequal in power and glory.

We believe that in the person of Jesus Christ the Divine and human natures are united, so that He is truly and properly God and truly and properly man.

We believe that our first parents were created in a state of innocency, but by their disobedience they lost their purity and happiness; and that in consequence of their fall all men have become sinners, totally depraved, and as such are justly exposed to the wrath of God.

We believe that the Lord Jesus Christ has, by His suffering and death, made an atonement for the whole world so that whosoever will may be saved.

We believe that repentance towards God, faith in our Lord Jesus Christ and regeneration by the Holy Spirit are necessary to salvation.

We believe that we are justified by grace, through faith in our Lord Jesus Christ; and that he that believeth hath the witness in himself.

We believe that continuance in a state of salvation depends upon continued obedient faith in Christ.

We believe that it is the privilege of all believers to be wholly sanctified, and that their whole spirit and soul and body may be preserved blameless unto the coming of our Lord Jesus Christ.

We believe in the immortality of the soul; in the resurrection of the body; in the general judgment at the end of the world; in the eternal happiness of the righteous; and in the endless punishment of the wicked.

THEREFORE

I will be responsive to the Holy Spirit's work and obedient to His leading in my life, growing in grace through worship, prayer, service and the reading of the Bible.

I will make the values of the Kingdom of God and not the values of the world the standard for my life.

I will uphold Christian integrity in every area of my life, allowing nothing in thought, word or deed that is unworthy, unclean, untrue, profane, dishonest or immoral.

I will maintain Christian ideals in all my relationships with others: my family and neighbours, my colleagues and fellow Salvationists, those to whom and for whom I am responsible, and the wider community.

I will uphold the sanctity of marriage and of family life.

I will be a faithful steward of my time and gifts, my money and possessions, my body, my mind and my spirit, knowing that I am accountable to God.

I will abstain from alcoholic drink, tobacco, the non-medical use of addictive drugs, gambling, pornography, the occult, and all else that could enslave the body or spirit.

I will be faithful to the purposes for which God raised up The Salvation Army, sharing the good news of Jesus Christ, endeavouring to win others to Him, and in His name caring for the needy and the disadvantaged.

I will be actively involved, as I am able, in the life, work, worship and witness of the corps, giving as large a proportion of my income as possible to support its ministries and the worldwide work of the Army.

I will be true to the principles and practices of The Salvation Army, loyal to its leaders, and I will show the spirit of Salvationism whether in times of popularity or persecution.

I now call upon all present to witness that I enter into this covenant and sign these articles of war of my own free will, convinced that the love of Christ, who died and now lives to save me, requires from me this devotion of my life to His service for the salvation of the whole world; and therefore do here declare my full determination, by God's help, to be a true soldier of The Salvation Army.

APPENDIX D
The Salvation Army and the Sacraments

The Significance of the Sacraments

Salvationists are well aware that most churches observe religious ceremonies called sacraments. The Roman Catholic Church observes seven. Most Protestant churches observe two: baptism and the Lord's Supper. Some churches add a third: foot washing. To most Protestants, a sacrament is either a symbol, a memorial, or a testimony; this means that Protestants feel that the sacraments are desirable and helpful but are not essential or necessary to salvation, although they may be required for church membership. The Quakers, however, do not see the necessity of the sacraments and do not observe them.

The Salvation Army in no way criticizes, and certainly does not condemn, any church for its practice. It is, however, The Salvation Army's firm conviction that the ceremonies commonly known as "the sacraments" are not necessary to salvation or essential to spiritual progress and, therefore, we do not observe them.

Biblical Ceremonies and Types

If it is anything, the religion of Jesus is intended to be a spiritual religion. For centuries, under the old covenant, the people of God had used ceremonies and types in their worship. There were the temple sacrifices, fasts and feasts, the rites of circumcision, and baptism for the converts to Judaism. But even long before Jesus came to earth, the prophets, such as

David, Jeremiah, and Amos, had to warn God's people that these ceremonies were meaningless, and actually unacceptable to God, if the spirit of the worshiper was not right. The ceremonies and the symbols were getting in the way of true worship and defeating their purpose.

It was with this in mind that Jesus declared plainly at the time of the new covenant: *"Yet a time is coming and has now come when the true worshipers will worship the Father in spirit and truth, for they are the kind of worshipers the Father seeks."* Then Jesus added: *"God is spirit, and His worshipers must worship in spirit and in truth"* (John 4:23-24). This is a profoundly important statement, foreseen by the prophets but made final by Jesus. A new hour, a new day, a new covenant had been made. And those who worship Him in spirit and truth, and not by rote, by ceremony, or by sacrament, are those whom the Father sees as His worshipers.

Fulfillment in Jesus

Furthermore, as Jesus Himself declared on numerous occasions, the types, the sacrifice, the ceremonies, the symbols, were fulfilled in Him. They need not be repeated or continued. The reason is that God Himself is a spiritual being. We Salvationists believe Jesus really meant what He said about fulfillment in Him.

Baptism

It is true that baptism has become a generally observed sacrament and a condition for church membership. Probably many of your friends in other churches have been baptized; perhaps you have been. To many this ceremony is based on the fact that Jesus Himself was baptized. Therefore, it is said we should "follow our Lord in baptism." An examination of the account in Matthew 3 will, however, indicate that John the Baptist recognized that his baptism by water was less important than, and was to be replaced by, the baptism of Jesus. His baptism is, of course, with the Holy Spirit, and water baptism is only a symbol. John told Jesus frankly that he needed this new baptism which Jesus only could give.

1.   *Jesus reinforced baptism by the Holy Spirit*. Jesus Himself rein-

forced this fact when He declared, just before His ascension: *"For John baptized with water, but in a few days you will be baptized with the Holy Spirit"* (Acts 1:5). We must remember that Jesus Himself did not baptize with water (John 4:2). Paul did not practice water baptism in his ministry as a rule, saying: *"Christ did not send me to baptize [with water], but to preach the gospel"* (1 Cor. 1:17). We, then, in the Army follow the teaching of John the Baptist, and the teaching and example of our Lord Jesus, and of the great evangelist Paul.

2. *Baptism is mentioned in the great commission.* It is apparent that Paul recognized the baptism mentioned in the great commission of Matthew 28:19-20 to be baptized with the Holy Spirit, for he explained in Ephesians 4:5 that there is *"one Lord, one faith"*; there is also *"one baptism."* He explained that the baptism is the baptism with the Holy Spirit, *"For we were all baptized by one Spirit into one body … and we were all given the one Spirit to drink"* (1 Cor. 12:13). With Paul and Jesus we would stress the only uniquely Christian baptism, which indeed was instituted by Christ: the baptism of the Holy Spirit.

Thus, The Salvation Army declares that the sacrament of water baptism is not necessary to salvation, nor commanded by Jesus.

The Lord's Supper

Some of your friends go to churches where they observe the Lord's Supper. Some of you may have gone to such churches and partaken of communion. It is, however, The Salvation Army's firm conviction that the ceremony known as the sacrament of the Lord's Supper is not essential to spiritual progress. The Church as a whole, although with many variations in form and meaning, celebrates a communion service which is commonly known as "the Lord's Supper" or "communion" but which others call "the mass." This service consists essentially of the eating of a small piece of bread, or water, in remembrance of the body of Christ, *"broken for you,"* and of drinking a small glass of grape juice (sometimes sweet and sometimes fermented) in remembrance of His blood *"which is shed for you."* The authority to do this is found in the six-word statement by Jesus at the time of the last Passover meal which He celebrated with His disciples, as recorded in Luke 22:19, and referred to in 1 Corinthians 11:24: *"Do this in remembrance of me."*

It is evident that Jesus did not, in fact, inaugurate here or establish a new sacramental ritual. Read these two verses: Luke 22:19-20. He first declared that the Passover supper, which was of the old covenant, was but a symbol of His own death which would seal the new covenant. In the Passover the Jews served unleavened bread and a cup of wine. So Jesus declared prophetically: *"This (the bread) is My body given for you ... This cup is the new covenant in My blood, which is poured out for you" (Luke 22:19-20).* Paul explained later: *"Christ, our Passover lamb, has been sacrificed"* (1 Cor. 5:7).

Jesus also gave a directive to remember His death whenever we eat and drink: *"Do this in memory of me."* The Salvationist does this when he "asks the blessing" before eating. Paul presented the same principle to the Corinthians, of remembering the Savior's death at their church meals (1 Cor. 11:33), which had come to be called *"the Lord's Supper"* (v. 20). But Church history bears out that not during Bible times of the first century was there developed a "Lord's Supper" in the form of a sacramental church observance. Nor is there any evidence that our Lord intended such an observance, nor did the early disciples practice it. This sacramental observance was a later development of the second or third century.

The Salvation Army's Position

The Salvation Army takes this position, with the Apostle Paul: *"The Kingdom of God is not a matter of eating and drinking, but of righteousness, peace, and joy in the Holy Spirit"* (Rom. 14:17). The Army gives heed to Jesus when He proclaims: *"A time is coming and has now come when the true worshipers will worship the Father in spirit and truth, for they are the kind of worshipers the Father seeks"* (John 4:23).

Excerpted from *Manual of Salvationism*

APPENDIX E

Statements from the International Spiritual Life Commission on the Sacraments

A Statement on Baptism

After full and careful consideration of The Salvation Army's understanding of, and approach to, the sacrament of water baptism, the International Spiritual Life Commission sets out the following points regarding the relationship between our soldier swearing-in and water baptism:

1. Only those who confess Jesus Christ as Saviour and Lord may be considered for soldiership in The Salvation Army.
2. Such a confession is confirmed by the gracious presence of God the Holy Spirit in the life of the believer and includes the call to discipleship.
3. In accepting the call to discipleship Salvationists promise to continue to be responsive to the Holy Spirit and to seek to grow in grace.
4. They also express publicly their desire to fulfil membership of Christ's Church on earth as soldiers of The Salvation Army.
5. The Salvation Army rejoices in the truth that all who are in Christ are baptised into the one body by the Holy Spirit (1 Corinthians 12:13).
6. It believes, in accordance with Scripture, that there is

one body and one Spirit ... one Lord, one faith, one
baptism; one God and Father of all, who is over all and
through all and in all (Ephesians 4:5-6).
7. The swearing-in of a soldier of The Salvation Army
    beneath the Trinitarian sign of the Army's flag acknowl-
    edges this truth.
8. It is a public response and witness to a life-changing
    encounter with Christ which has already taken place, as
    is the water baptism practised by some other Christians.
9. The Salvation Army acknowledges that there are many
    worthy ways of publicly witnessing to having been bap-
    tised into Christ's body by the Holy Spirit and express-
    ing a desire to be his disciple.
10. The swearing-in of a soldier should be followed by a
    lifetime of continued obedient faith in Christ.

A Statement on Holy Communion

After full and careful consideration of The Salvation Army's understanding of, and approach to, the sacrament of Holy Communion, the
International Spiritual Life Commission sets out the following points:

1. God's grace is freely and readily accessible to all people at all
    times and in all places.
2. No particular outward observance is necessary to inward
    grace.
3. The Salvation Army believes that unity of the Spirit exists
    within diversity and rejoices in the freedom of the Spirit in
    expressions of worship.
4. When Salvationists attend other Christian gatherings in
    which a form of Holy Communion is included, they may
    partake if they choose to do so and if the host Church allows.
5. Christ is the one true Sacrament, and sacramental living—
    Christ living in us and through us—is at the heart of Chris-
    tian holiness and discipleship.

6. Throughout its history The Salvation Army has kept Christ's atoning sacrifice at the centre of its corporate worship.
7. The Salvation Army rejoices in its freedom to celebrate Christ's real presence at all meals and in all meetings, and in its opportunity to explore in life together the significance of the simple meals shared by Jesus and his friends and by the first Christians.
8. Salvationists are encouraged to use the love feast and develop creative means of hallowing meals in home and corps with remembrance of the Lord's sacrificial love.
9. The Salvation Army encourages the development of resources for fellowship meals, which will vary according to culture, without ritualising particular words or actions.
10. In accordance with normal Salvation Army practice, such remembrances and celebrations, where observed, will not become established rituals, nor will frequency be prescribed.

Excerpted from *Called to be God's People*

APPENDIX F

Conditions of Adherency to The Salvation Army

1. Must be over 15 years of age.

2. Must be of good character and standing.

3. Must not be an active member of another religious body.

4. Will agree to:

   a. Support financially, and in any way, the work of The Salvation Army.

   b. Attend as regularly as possible the meetings of The Salvation Army

   c. Look to The Salvation Army officer to conduct the ceremonies of marriage, dedication of children, and funerals.

   d. Have his or her name entered on government or religious census records as an adherent of The Salvation Army.

NOTES

[1] *Alcoholics Anonymous* (New York: Alcoholics Anonymous World Services, Inc., 1976), 46.

[2] Craig Nakken, *The Addictive Personality* (Center City, MN: Hazelden, 1996) 5, 15.

[3] *Alcoholics Anonymous*, 63.

[4] Robert Street, *Called to Be God's People* (London: Salvation Books, 1999) 9.

[5] Ibid.

[6] Ibid.

[7] Ibid., 17.

[8] Ibid.

[9] Ibid., 19.

[10] Ibid., 20.

[11] Ibid., 26-27.

[12] *Alcoholics Anonymous*, 58.

[13] Street, *Called to Be God's People*, 35.

[14] Ibid., 43.

[15] Ibid., 45-46.

[16] Ibid., 50.

[17] Ibid., 7.

[18] Ibid., 49.

[19] *Alcoholics Anonymous*, 64.

[20] Ibid., 76.

[21] Street, *Called to be God's People*, 59.

[22] Ibid., 55.

[23] Ibid., 73.

[24] Ibid., 74.
[25] *Alcoholics Anonymous*, 83.
[26] Street, *Called to be God's People*, 76.
[27] *Alcoholics Anonymous*, 84-85.
[28] Chuck C., *A New Pair of Glasses* (Irvine, CA: New-Look Publishing Company, 1986) 109.
[29] *Alcoholics Anonymous*, 85.
[30] Street, *Called to be God's People*, 84.
[31] Ibid., 81.
[32] *Alcoholics Anonymous*, 58.
[33] Street, *Called to be God's People*, 84.
[34] Ibid., 79.
[35] Ibid., 85.
[36] Ibid., 88.
[37] Ibid., 87.
[38] *Alcoholics Anonymous*, 64.
[39] Ibid., 68.
[40] Ibid., 84.
[41] Street, *Called to be God's People*, 94.
[42] Ibid., 94-95.
[43] Ibid., 87.
[44] Ibid., 98.
[45] Ibid., 100.
[46] Ibid., 101.